THE LEADERSHIP COACHING SOURCEBOOK

A GUIDE TO THE EXECUTIVE COACHING LITERATURE

THE LEADERSHIP COACHING SOURCEBOOK

A GUIDE TO THE EXECUTIVE COACHING LITERATURE

Johnathan K. Nelson
Lisa A. Boyce
Gina Hernez-Broome
Katherine Ely
Gia A. DiRosa

Center for Creative Leadership
Greensboro, North Carolina

The Center for Creative Leadership is an international, nonprofit educational institution founded in 1970 to advance the understanding, practice, and development of leadership for the benefit of society worldwide. As a part of this mission, it publishes books and reports that aim to contribute to a general process of inquiry and understanding in which ideas related to leadership are raised, exchanged, and evaluated. The ideas presented in its publications are those of the author or authors.

CENTER FOR CREATIVE LEADERSHIP
WWW.CCL.ORG

Center for
Creative
Leadership®

CCL Stock No. 357
© 2011 Center for Creative Leadership

Published by CCL Press
Sylvester Taylor, Director of Assessments, Tools, and Publications
Peter Scisco, Manager, Publication Development
Stephen Rush, Senior Editor
Karen Lewis, Associate Editor

Library of Congress Cataloging-in-Publication Data

The leadership coaching sourcebook : a guide to the executive coaching literature / Johnathan K. Nelson ... [et al.] — 1st ed.
    p. cm.
  ISBN 978-1-60491-087-2 (print on demand) — ISBN 978-1-60491-088-9 (e-book)
1. Executive coaching. 2. Executives—Training of. 3. Leadership—Study and teaching.
I. Nelson, Johnathan K.
  HD30.4.L395 2011
  658.4'07124—dc22
                                                            2010054239

Table of Contents

Overview

Despite the fact that executive coaching is a relatively new means of leadership development, interest in executive coaching is strong (Kampa-Kokesch & Anderson, 2001). Executive coaching is an increasingly popular means for developing organizational leaders. This interest is reflected in the rapid growth in the use of executive coaching in organizations, as well as the growth in the popular press including books and articles related to executive coaching (Sherman & Freas, 2004). Although scholarly research on executive coaching is growing, it lags behind practice and is considerably disjointed.

The purpose of this sourcebook is to provide a resource for both practitioners and researchers interested in gaining or updating their understanding of the current state of the executive coaching field and to enable them to do so in a systematic manner. By focusing on key research and practices in the executive coaching literature, this sourcebook provides not only a mechanism for consolidating our thinking about leadership coaching issues but also a succinct reference for building future research efforts. As such, this sourcebook will be a useful means for facilitating evidence-based management practices in the application of executive coaching. Researchers and practitioners who are new to executive coaching will find this a helpful introduction to the field, and those with more experience will find a useful reference and quick update of emerging trends in current research and practice.

This sourcebook is divided into seven sections. The first section describes how to use the sourcebook to fit your individual needs. A brief definition and historical overview of executive coaching is provided in Section 2, followed by an overview of the Leadership Coaching Framework used to organize the articles presented in Section 3. Section 4 describes how articles were selected for inclusion in the sourcebook. Section 5 summarizes emerging themes from each category of articles considered as well as future directions. Section 6 includes the outline for each article included in the sourcebook and highlights the purpose(s), methodology, and implications for each article. Finally, in Section 7 we compiled a list of additional resources that we and our colleagues have found useful; although this is not comprehensive, particularly as the field of executive coaching continues to grow, we felt a singular consolidated listing would be a useful resource for our readers.

Section 1. Using This Sourcebook

This sourcebook is designed to both provide an introduction to the topic of executive coaching and help guide experienced researchers and practitioners to literature most relevant for their needs. Literature on executive coaching has grown substantially since the annotated bibliography compiled by Douglas and Morley (2000). Due to the growing size and breadth of this literature, rather than simply providing an updated annotated bibliography, this sourcebook strategically compiles key publications as a means to highlight the state of leadership coaching.

This sourcebook can be used in a variety of ways. First, Section 2 provides a brief overview of the past and current state of the executive coaching literature. This material provides a brief synopsis for individuals who have limited or dated knowledge of executive coaching and wish to gain a greater understanding of the major issues in the literature. In addition to this general overview, Section 5 presents a summary of the current literature as well as discussion of the major factors in leadership coaching according to the framework provided in Section 4. We encourage readers to examine Figures 1 and 2 for an overview of the issues and corresponding articles.

For individuals wishing to develop deeper knowledge of a particular topic related to executive coaching, outlines of topic-specific articles are provided in Section 6. Although not intended to replace the original articles, these outlines were designed to help you identify the articles most relevant to your needs. Additionally, each article has been assigned codes to help readers efficiently identify the type of methodology employed, particularly useful introductions of a topic, number of citations included, number of pages, and the type of article (for example, conceptual or empirical). Table 1 provides a list and definitions of the codes, and Table 2 maps each article according to these codes.

Thus, this sourcebook can be read in its entirety to provide a comprehensive overview of current coaching publications, or it can be used to identify resources specific to an individual reader's needs.

Table 1. Definitions of codes assigned to articles

Code	Definition
Article Type	
T1	Conceptual article: includes propositions or arguments based on theory
T2	Research article: tests one or more specific hypotheses
T3	Literature review: review of relevant literature with no propositions or hypothesis testing
T4	Case study: based on a limited number of personal experiences; may include some basic descriptive statistics
T5	Viewpoint: provides a point of view on leadership coaching
Introduction	
I	Article includes an extremely thorough, detailed, and well-written introduction to executive coaching
Methodology	
M	Article describes a methodologically rigorous study design in enough detail to facilitate replication
Citations	
C#	Number of citations referenced in the article
Page Number	
P#	Total page length of the article

Table 2. Summary of all articles coded

Reference	Title	Article Type	Intro	Method	Citations	Pages
Ahern (2005)	Coaching professionalism and provider size	5			1	6
Alvey & Barclay (2007)	The characteristics of dyadic trust in executive coaching	2			36	9
Armstrong, Melser, & Tooth (2007)	Executive coaching effectiveness: A pathway to self-efficacy	2			53	30
Axelrod (2005)	Executive growth along the adult development curve	4			14	8
Barner & Higgins (2007)	Understanding implicit models that guide the coaching process	1			34	9
Baron & Morin (2009)	The coach-coachee relationship in executive coaching: A field study	2	X	X	77	21
Baron & Morin (2010)	The impact of executive coaching on self-efficacy related to management soft-skills	2	X		99	21
Berman & Brandt (2006)	Executive coaching and consulting: "Different strokes for different folks"	1			34	17
Blackman (2006)	Factors that contribute to the effectiveness of business coaching: The coachees' perspective	2			21	7
Blukert (2005a)	Critical factors in executive coaching—the coaching relationship	1			4	5
Blukert (2005b)	The foundation of a psychological approach to executive coaching	1	X		14	8
Bono, Purvanova, Towler, & Peterson (2009)	A survey of executive coaching practices	2	X		52	43
Boyce & Hernez-Broome (2010)	E-coaching: Considerations of leadership coaching in a virtual environment	1	X	X	65	34
Boyce, Jackson, & Neal (2010)	Building successful leadership coaching relationships: Examining impact of matching criteria in a leadership coaching program	2	X	X	57	NA
Carr (2008)	Coach referral services: Do they work?	1			5	6
Cocivera & Cronshaw (2004)	Action frame theory as a practical framework for the executive coaching process	1			13	12

Table 2. Summary of all articles coded (cont.)

Reference	Title	Article Type	Intro	Method	Citations	Pages
Coutu & Kauffman (2009)	What can coaches do for you?	2			0	7
Dagley (2006)	Human resources professionals' perceptions of executive coaching: Efficacy, benefits and return on investment	2	X	X	11	10
Dean & Meyer (2002)	Executive coaching: In search of a model	1			20	14
de Haan, Bertie, Day, & Sills (in press)	Critical moments of clients of coaching: Towards a 'client model' of executive coaching	2		X	46	46
de Haan, Culpin, & Curd (2011)	Executive coaching in practice: What determines helpfulness for clients of coaching?	2		X	29	37
De Meuse, Dai, & Lee (2009)	Evaluating the effectiveness of executive coaching: Beyond ROI?	3	X		71	17
Driscoll (2005)	E-mentoring and e-coaching	5	X		6	20
Ducharme (2004)	The cognitive-behavioral approach to executive coaching	1			29	11
Ely, Boyce, Nelson, Zaccaro, Hernez-Broome, & Whyman (2010)	Evaluating leadership coaching: A review and integrated framework	1	X		113	15
Evers, Brouwers, & Tomic (2006)	A quasi-experimental study on management coaching effectiveness	2			19	9
Feldman & Lankau (2005)	Executive coaching: A review and agenda for future research	3	X		75	19
Garman, Whiston, & Zlatoper (2000)	Media perceptions of executive coaching and the formal preparation of coaches	2			10	5
Goldsmith (2006)	E-coaching: Using the new technology to develop tomorrow's leaders	5			0	8
Grant, Curtayne, & Burton (2009)	Executive coaching enhances goal attainment, resilience and work-place well-being: A randomised controlled study	2			52	12
Gyllensten & Palmer (2007)	The coaching relationship: An interpretative phenomenological analysis	2	X		20	10

Table 2. Summary of all articles coded (cont.)

Reference	Title	Article Type	Intro	Method	Citations	Pages
Hakim (2003)	Virtual coaching: Learning, like time, stops for no one	5			0	3
Hall, Otazo, & Hollenbeck (1999)	Behind closed doors: What really happens in executive coaching	2			0	14
Hamilton & Scandura (2003)	E-mentoring: Implications for organizational learning and development in a wired world	5	X		0	15
Hernez-Broome & Hughes (2004)	Leadership development: Past, present and future	1			45	8
Hollenbeck (2002)	Coaching executives: Individual leadership development	5	X		24	30
Homan & Miller (2008)	Developing master coaching skills	5			1	28
Hooijberg & Lane (2009)	Using multisource feedback coaching effectively in executive education	2	X		23	11
Jay (2003)	Understanding how to leverage executive coaching	5	X		11	13
Jones, Rafferty, & Griffin (2006)	The executive coaching trend: Towards more flexible executives	2			33	13
Joo (2005)	Executive coaching: A conceptual framework from an integrative review of practice and research	1		X	60	26
Kampa-Kokesch & Anderson (2001)	Executive coaching: A comprehensive review of the literature	3	X	X	90	23
Kaspirin, Single, Single, & Muller (2003)	Building a better bridge: Testing e-training to improve e-mentoring programmes in higher education	2	X	X	21	12
Kilburg (2004)	When shadows fall: Using psychodynamic approaches in executive coaching	1			43	23
Knouse (2001)	Virtual mentors: Mentoring on the Internet	3			27	7
Kochanowski, Seifert, & Yukl (2010)	Using coaching to enhance the effects of behavioral feedback to managers	2		X	30	7

Table 2. Summary of all articles coded (cont.)

Reference	Title	Article Type	Intro	Method	Citations	Pages
Kombarakaran, Yang, Baker, & Fernandes (2008)	Executive coaching: It works!	2			19	13
Latham (2007)	Theory and research on coaching practices	5			20	3
Levenson (2009)	Measuring and maximizing the business impact of executive coaching	4	X		59	19
Liljenstrand & Nebeker (2008)	Coaching services: A look at coaches, clients, and practices	2	X		32	21
Linley, Woolston, & Biswas-Diener (2009)	Strengths coaching with leaders	1			31	12
Lowman (2005)	Executive coaching: The road to dodoville needs paving with more than good assumptions	3			16	7
Mallen, Day, & Green (2003)	Online versus face-to-face conversations: An examination of relational and discourse variables	2	X	X	26	9
McDermott, Levenson, & Newton (2007)	What coaching can and cannot do for your organization	2			0	8
McKenna & Davis (2009)	Hidden in plain sight: The active ingredients of executive coaching	1	X		33	17
Nowack (2009)	Leveraging multirater feedback to facilitate successful behavioral change	1			78	18
O'Broin & Palmer (2006)	The coach-client relationship and contributions made by the coach in improving coaching outcome	3	X		43	5
O'Broin & Palmer (2009)	Co-creating an optimal coaching alliance: A cognitive behavioural coaching perspective	1			65	11
Orenstein (2002)	Executive coaching: It's not just about the executive	1	X		37	20

Table 2. Summary of all articles coded (cont.)

Reference	Title	Article Type	Intro	Method	Citations	Pages
Orenstein (2006)	Measuring executive coaching efficacy? The answer was right here all the time	4			18	11
Passmore (2007)	An integrative model for executive coaching	1			45	12
Passmore & Gibbes (2007)	The state of executive coaching research: What does the current literature tell us and what's next for coaching research?	3	X		65	13
Passmore, Rawle-Cope, Gibbes, & Holloway (2006)	MBTI® types and executive coaching	2			8	9
Perkins (2009)	How executive coaching can change leader behavior and improve meeting effectiveness: An exploratory study	2, 4		X	46	20
Pulley (2006)	Blended coaching	4, 5			9	32
Quick & Macik-Frey (2004)	Behind the mask: Coaching through deep interpersonal communication	1			31	8
Renner (2007)	Coaching abroad: Insights about assets	5			27	14
Riddle, Zan, & Kuzmycz (2009)	Five myths about executive coaching	1			0	3
Scoular & Linley (2006)	Coaching, goal-setting and personality type: What matters?	2, 5			13	3
Sherin & Caiger (2004)	Rational-emotive behavior therapy: A behavioral change model for executive coaching?	1			42	9
Smither, London, Flautt, Vargas, & Kucine (2003)	Can working with an executive coach improve multisource feedback ratings over time? A quasi-experimental field study	2	X	X	41	21
Sparrow (2008)	Finding a coach: The perfect match	1, 5			0	6
Stern (2004)	Executive coaching: A working definition	1			11	9
Stevens (2005)	Executive coaching from the executive's perspective	4			16	11

Table 2. Summary of all articles coded (cont.)

Reference	Title	Article Type	Intro	Method	Citations	Pages
Stewart, Palmer, Wilkin, & Kerrin (2008)	The influence of character: Does personality impact coaching success?	2			35	10
Sue-Chan & Latham (2004)	The relative effectiveness of external, peer, and self-coaches	2	X	X	60	19
Thach (2002)	The impact of executive coaching and 360 feedback on leadership effectiveness	2		X	31	10
Ting & Hart (2003)	Formal coaching	3	X		0	34
Turner & Goodrich (2010)	The case for eclecticism in executive coaching: Application to challenging assignments	4	X		63	16
Wasylyshyn (2003)	Executive coaching: An outcome study	2			9	13
Wycherley & Cox (2008)	Factors in the selection and matching of executive coaches in organizations	1	X		62	15

Section 2. The Past and Current State of Executive Coaching

Executive coaching has witnessed an increase in popularity in both practice and research in the past two decades (Dagley, 2006; Passmore 2007). Although coaching and leader development efforts have been used in organizations for the past half century (Day, 2001; Kampa-Kokesch & Anderson, 2001), the term *executive coaching* was first coined in the 1980s in order to reduce the punitive stigma associated with coaching. However, practices were still predominantly corrective in nature and aimed at ineffective leaders (Kampa-Kokesch & Anderson, 2001). The practice of executive coaching substantially increased in the early 1990s, as faltering organizations attributed organizational problems to poor leadership. As a result, coaching maintained a punitive connotation (Feldman & Lankau, 2005) for another decade.

Only within the past decade has executive coaching evolved into a developmental opportunity and come to be perceived in a positive light for leaders (Feldman & Lankau, 2005). Today, coaches work closely with executives on long-term goals, daily activities, and interpersonal skills (Dean & Meyer, 2002; Hernez-Broome & Hughes, 2004; Jay, 2003). The success and subsequent demand for executive coaching has created an enormous growth in the number of professional coaches and coaching programs in organizations (Day, 2001; Dean & Meyer, 2002; Feldman & Lankau, 2005; Hernez-Broome & Hughes, 2004).

Despite the advent of executive coaching practices, the literature provides little consensus on a definition of executive coaching. However, the field appears to be reaching a convergence regarding the core components, as evidenced by several articles agreeing on what coaching is and what it is not. Executive coaching is, at its most fundamental level, a purposeful one-on-one relationship for developing effective leaders (Day, 2001; Dean & Meyer, 2002; Feldman & Lankau, 2005; Jay, 2005; Joo, 2005; Stern, 2004). Leadership coaching is *not* mentoring, training, consulting, or therapy (Feldman & Lankau, 2005; Hollenbeck, 2002; Kampa-Kokesch & Anderson, 2001; Passmore & Gibbes, 2007; Stern, 2004). We are partial to the Center for Creative Leadership (CCL) definition: "a practice in which the coach and coachee collaborate to assess and understand the developmental task, challenge current constraints while exploring new possibilities, and ensure accountability and support for reaching goals and sustaining development" (Ting & Hart, 2003, p. 116).

Similar to this definition, a range of terms are used to describe the participants in a coaching engagement. To be more comprehensive, we elected to incorporate many of these terms and to generally use them interchangeably. For example, executive coaching may also be referred to as leadership coaching, and clients may also be referred to as coachees.

The literature indicates several common goals that characterize executive coaching. Three predominant objectives of executive coaching are (a) developing self-awareness, (b) overcoming behaviors that limit personal and organizational success, and (c) building skills, particularly for high potentials, to support dynamic organizational needs (Anderson, Frankovelgia, & Hernez-Broome, 2009; Day, 2001; Dean & Meyer, 2002; Jay, 2005). Although these objectives focus on the individual, coaching also considers the individual as part of a larger system (Orenstein, 2002) and ultimately aims to foster organizational-level goals (Stern, 2004). Supplementary objectives often include increasing motivation and interpersonal skills (Dean & Meyer, 2002; Jay, 2005).

Two recent trends are expanding coaching objectives. First, changes in organizational functioning have elicited an increased need for both interpersonal skills and effective adaptability beyond simple business knowledge (Joo, 2005; Kampa-Kokesch & Anderson, 2001). Organizations have responded to these changes by taking a more vested interest in their human capital by incorporating coaching across human resource practices and growing a coaching culture (Anderson et al., 2009; Day, 2001). Second, coaching has received an increasing amount of attention from the fields of business and psychology (Day, 2001; Dean & Meyer, 2002; Kampa-Kokesch & Anderson, 2005). As a result, coaching practices are gaining an industrial-and-organizational-psychology perspective and the field is moving toward a science-practitioner model (McKenna & Davis, 2009).

Although research has responded to the trend, as evidenced by an increase in theoretical and empirical articles, much of the literature is still lagging practice, and many specifics of coaching theory and application remain unexplored (Feldman & Lankau, 2005; Hernez-Broome & Boyce, 2010; Joo, 2005; Kampa-Kokesch & Anderson, 2001). The following sections of the sourcebook will examine the state of the literature in more detail. Needless to say, executive coaching is an important and fruitful avenue for research and the development of evidence-based practices.

Section 3. Introduction of the Leadership Coaching Framework

Coaching is a complex social system in which many factors interact to impact the success of a coaching program. Systems theory (Katz & Kahn, 1978) provides us with a tool to examine such a complex system by allowing us to frame the key variables that work together to produce effective results. The three central components of an I-P-O model are the *input* or the external factors that enter the system, the *process* or the actions taken upon the input materials, and the *output* or the results of the process. The Leadership Coaching Framework (Boyce & Hernez-Broome, 2007; see Figure 1, p. 14) uses an I-P-O framework to frame the key issues relevant to executive coaching, including coach and client characteristics (input), the coaching process, and coaching outcomes (output). Additional components that may moderate or impact the relationships between the input and process include the coach-client match, organizational support, and the medium through which coaching occurs.

Although this framework is presented in *Advancing Executive Coaching: Setting the Course for Successful Leadership Development* (Hernez-Broome & Boyce, 2010), we provide a brief review of this model here as an organizing strategy for the sourcebook. The six components illustrated in Figure 1 were employed to select, examine, understand, and summarize the published literature. In addition, the framework provides a mechanism for future research to systematically consider, investigate, and promote evidenced-based coaching, as well as a tool for practitioners to systematically examine and develop coaching practices.

Coach and Client Characteristics

The coach and client enter a coaching engagement with preexisting characteristics, such as a level of readiness, motivation, and personality. Level of readiness implies that coaches have varying degrees of experience and range and depth of competencies, and differing perspectives or philosophies about coaching itself. Similarly, clients bring different levels of experience, skills, and needs to the coaching process. Coach and client motivation as well as their unique personality differences are also particularly relevant, as they influence not only their behaviors toward particular goals but also their emotional and cognitive processing, such as with feedback.

Coach-Client Match

In addition to understanding the coach and client, the match or fit between coach and client is critical to the partnership and the success of the

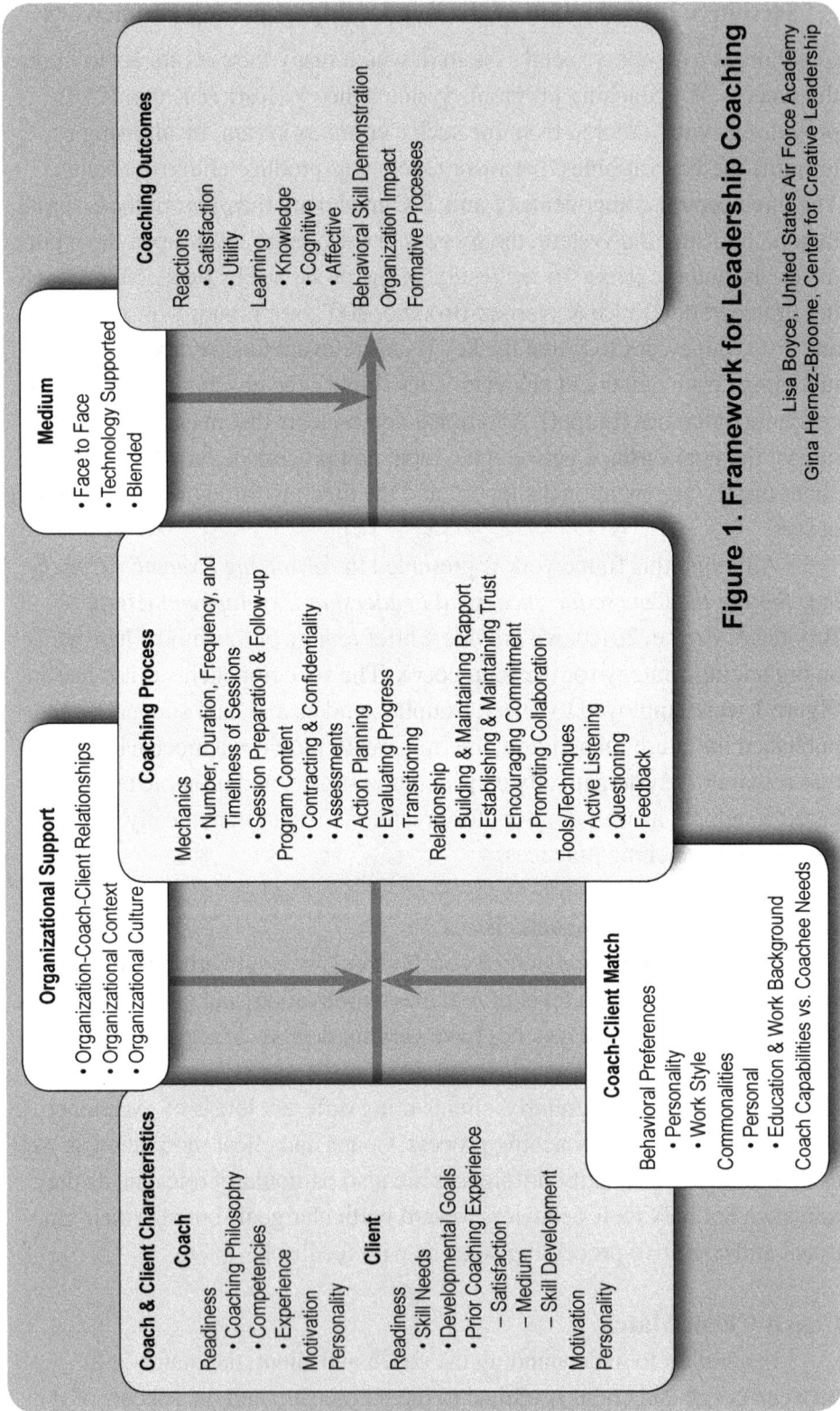

Coach & Client Characteristics

Coach

Readiness
• Coaching Philosophy
• Competencies
• Experience
Motivation
Personality

Client

Readiness
• Skill Needs
• Developmental Goals
• Prior Coaching Experience
  – Satisfaction
  – Medium
  – Skill Development
Motivation
Personality

Organizational Support
• Organization-Coach-Client Relationships
• Organizational Context
• Organizational Culture

Coaching Process

Mechanics
• Number, Duration, Frequency, and Timeliness of Sessions
• Session Preparation & Follow-up
Program Content
• Contracting & Confidentiality
• Assessments
• Action Planning
• Evaluating Progress
• Transitioning
Relationship
• Building & Maintaining Rapport
• Establishing & Maintaining Trust
• Encouraging Commitment
• Promoting Collaboration
Tools/Techniques
• Active Listening
• Questioning
• Feedback

Coach-Client Match

Behavioral Preferences
• Personality
• Work Style
Commonalities
• Personal
• Education & Work Background
Coach Capabilities vs. Coachee Needs

Medium
• Face to Face
• Technology Supported
• Blended

Coaching Outcomes

Reactions
• Satisfaction
• Utility
Learning
• Knowledge
• Cognitive
• Affective
Behavioral Skill Demonstration
Organization Impact
Formative Processes

Figure 1. Framework for Leadership Coaching

Lisa Boyce, United States Air Force Academy
Gina Hernez-Broome, Center for Creative Leadership

coaching engagement. Possible factors to consider when aligning coaches with clients include compatibility in personality preferences, commonalities in professional and personal values, interests and experiences, and coach credibility referent to the client's needs. Personality preferences refer to the compatibility between coach and client personality and work/learning styles, which may impact coaching processes ranging from establishing initial rapport to later stretch activities. Commonalities capture the underlying features that attract individuals to each other and support communication and relationship development and maintenance, such as demographic variables (for example, gender, race, and age), work and education backgrounds, and personal interests and activities. Credibility encompasses the extent to which the coach possesses the specific capabilities and experiences to support the client's perceived and real needs.

Organizational Support

Leadership coaching does not occur in a vacuum; organizational influences need to also be considered in coaching research and practice. The relationships between key organization stakeholders, coach, and client, as well as the organizational context and culture, may affect the coaching process, such as program mechanics, contracting and confidentiality, and the effectiveness of the assessment tools and action strategies. These organizational factors are expected to impact the effects of individual coach and client characteristics on the coaching processes, such as integrating client goals and action plans into the work environment, fostering learning transfer, and sustaining the developmental process.

Coaching Process

The coaching process is partitioned into four major subprocesses: mechanics, program content, relationship, and tools and techniques. Mechanics focus on the logistics of the coaching session (for example, number, duration, frequency, timeliness or responsiveness of sessions, and session prep and closure, including preparing an agenda, completing homework, and documenting the meeting). Although individual coaches may identify with certain models of coaching, most coaching programs include similar content or elements, which include contracting, establishing confidentiality, assessments, action planning, evaluating progress, and transitioning. The four key processes associated with the client-coach relationship are building and maintaining rapport, establishing and maintaining trust, encouraging commitment, and promoting collaboration. These four social constructs involve a mutual responsibility between a coach and client. Finally, tools and techniques include the actual coaching behaviors (for example, active listening, questioning, and feedback).

Medium

With the majority of coaches coaching in mediums other than face-to-face using tools ranging from e-mail to virtual simulations, the impact of the coaching medium is of growing interest. Adding technology to the already unique nature of a one-on-one coaching process increases the complexity of the interaction. Therefore, the medium by which coaching is delivered (face-to face coaching, technology supported, or blended delivery) is framed as moderating the relationship between the coaching process and coaching outcomes.

Coaching Outcomes

Assessing coaching outcomes is critical to practitioners and researchers in determining the effectiveness of coaching programs and processes. The framework considers leadership coaching outcomes from a training perspective but also acknowledges the unique aspects of coaching as a learning and development intervention. Therefore, relevant coaching outcomes include the traditional summative training criteria, such as reactions, learning and behavioral skill demonstration, and organizational impact (Kirkpatrick, 1994), as well as formative or process criteria. The broad factors encourage the tailoring of criteria to meet coaching's specific and evolving purposes, such as incorporating cognitive and affective outcomes (for example, cognitive flexibility and self-efficacy). We encourage you to review Ely et al. (2010) for a more complete discussion of coaching evaluation within the Leadership Coaching Framework, as the distinctive aspects of coaching present additional challenges for assessing outcomes for both practice and research.

Summary

The Leadership Coaching Framework consists of six components that support the examination of key coaching factors. Further, the framework assembles key factors within the components to emphasize their relationships and interconnections. The framework, therefore, provides a useful structure to examine the coaching literature to increase our understanding of the state of the field, generate methodical research, and better inform and guide practice.

Section 4. Article Selection Criteria

As the purpose of the sourcebook is to provide an overview of the state of the executive coaching literature as well as guide readers to specific exemplar articles, we determined three necessary steps for identifying and selecting articles. First, relevant databases were identified. Second, the parameters for identifying relevant articles were defined. And third, the articles were reviewed and selected for inclusion in the sourcebook.

Various databases were used to identify relevant sources, including Psych-INFO, ABI-Inform, and Google Scholar. Executive coaching and leadership coaching were included as search terms, in combination with specific terms from the Leadership Coaching Framework, to identify articles for each specific component of the model. We also examined coaching-specific journals, which are not in the traditional databases.

When we were selecting articles from these publications to be reviewed as well as included in the sourcebook, a number of selection criteria were considered. First, priority was given to more recent articles, particularly those published since the annotated bibliography by Douglas and Morley in 2000. Additionally, articles identified as having a high impact on the field, such as being cited in numerous other sources, were prioritized over articles having less of an impact. Third, any review articles that have been published to date were included in order to point readers toward other valuable executive coaching resources. Further, an effort was made to include scholarly research articles as well as high-quality practitioner resources.

Finally, we chose to limit the number of articles to make the sourcebook as manageable and practically useful as possible. Therefore, ten to fifteen articles with a primary focus on each of the six components of the Leadership Coaching Framework—coach and client characteristics, coach-client match, organizational support, coaching process, medium, and coaching outcomes—were selected for inclusion. The articles representing each section of the Leadership Coaching Framework are presented in Figure 2 (p. 18). Some components of the framework contain more publications than others, as more than one topic was often addressed in an article, therefore an article may be listed in multiple locations. A total of eighty-one articles are included in the sourcebook (Section 6).

As the coaching literature becomes more expansive, we acknowledge that some worthwhile publications on executive coaching may not have been identified and therefore that some exemplar articles may not be included in this sourcebook. Further, we did not intend the sourcebook to be a comprehensive reference list of every leadership-coaching-related publication.

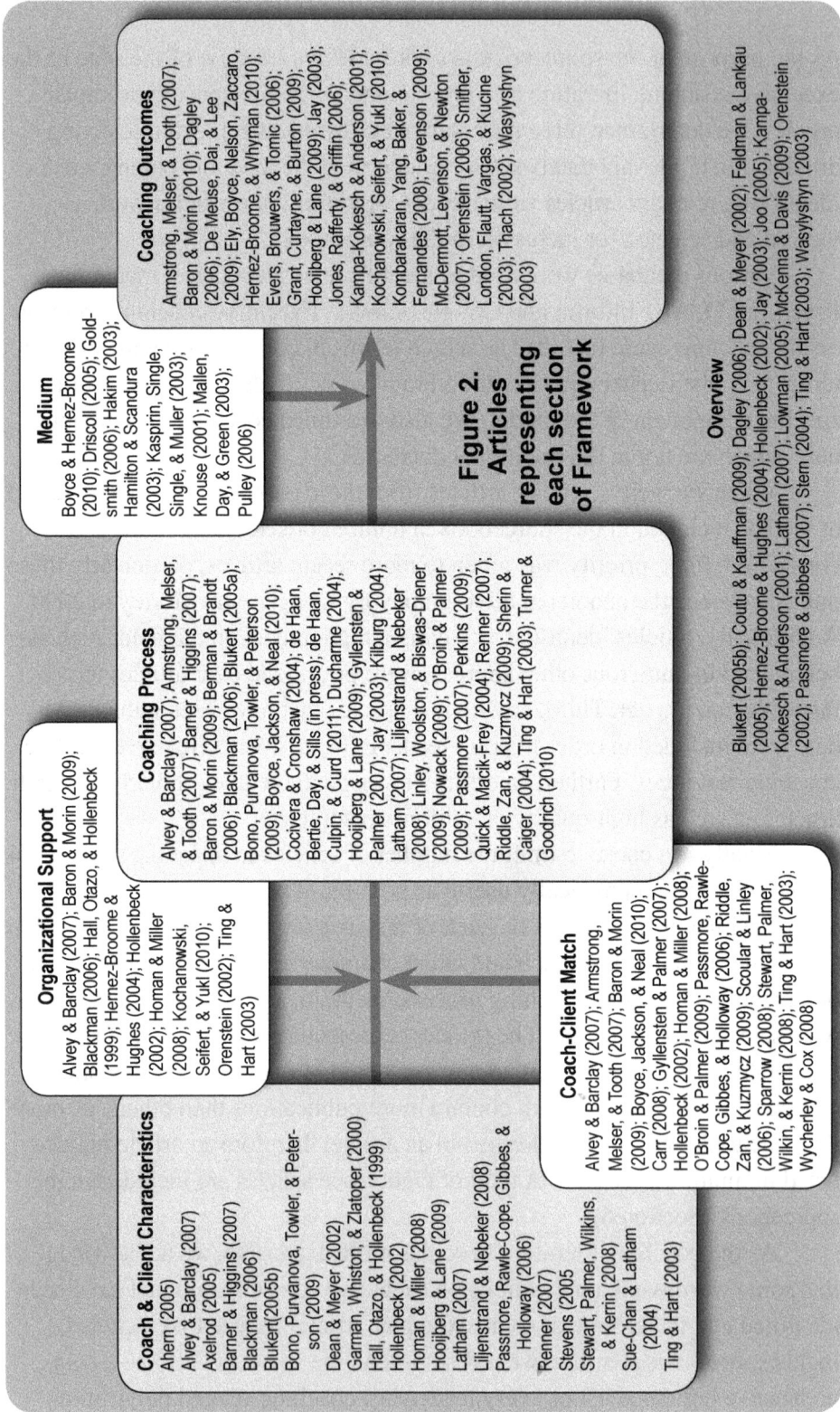

Coaching Outcomes
Armstrong, Melser, & Tooth (2007); Baron & Morin (2010); Dagley (2006); De Meuse, Dai, & Lee (2009); Ely, Boyce, Nelson, Zaccaro, Hernez-Broome, & Whyman (2010); Evers, Brouwers, & Tomic (2006); Grant, Curtayne, & Burton (2009); Hooijberg & Lane (2009); Jay (2003); Jones, Rafferty, & Griffin (2006); Kampa-Kokesch & Anderson (2001); Kochanowski, Seifert, & Yukl (2010); Kombarakaran, Yang, Baker, & Fernandes (2008); Levenson (2009); McDermott, Levenson, & Newton (2007); Orenstein (2006); Smither, London, Flautt, Vargas, & Kucine (2003); Thach (2002); Wasylyshyn (2003)

Medium
Boyce & Hernez-Broome (2010); Driscoll (2005); Goldsmith (2006); Hakim (2003); Hamilton & Scandura (2003); Kasprin, Single, Single, & Muller (2003); Knouse (2001); Mallen, Day, & Green (2003); Pulley (2006)

Figure 2. Articles representing each section of Framework

Coaching Process
Alvey & Barclay (2007); Armstrong, Melser, & Tooth (2007); Barner & Higgins (2007); Baron & Morin (2009); Berman & Brandt (2006); Blackman (2006); Blukert (2005a); Bono, Purvanova, Towler, & Peterson (2009); Boyce, Jackson, & Neal (2010); Cocivera & Cronshaw (2004); de Haan, Bertie, Day, & Sills (in press); de Haan, Culpin, & Curd (2011); Ducharme (2004); Gyllensten & Hooijberg & Lane (2009); Gyllensten & Palmer (2007); Jay (2003); Kilburg (2004); Latham (2007); Lijenstrand & Nebeker (2008); Linley, Woolston, & Biswas-Diener (2009); Nowack (2009); O'Broin & Palmer (2009); Passmore (2007); Perkins (2009); Quick & Macik-Frey (2004); Renner (2007); Riddle, Zan, & Kuzmycz (2009); Sherin & Caiger; Ting & Hart (2003); Turner & Goodrich (2010)

Organizational Support
Alvey & Barclay (2007); Baron & Morin (2009); Blackman (2006); Hall, Otazo, & Hollenbeck (1999); Hernez-Broome & Hughes (2004); Hollenbeck (2002); Homan & Miller (2008); Kochanowski, Seifert, & Yukl (2010); Orenstein (2002); Ting & Hart (2003)

Coach-Client Match
Alvey & Barclay (2007); Armstrong, Melser, & Tooth (2007); Baron & Morin (2009); Boyce, Jackson, & Neal (2010); Carr (2008); Gyllensten & Palmer (2007); Hollenbeck (2002); Homan & Miller (2008); O'Broin & Palmer (2009); Passmore, Rawle-Cope, Gibbes, & Holloway (2006); Riddle, Zan, & Kuzmycz (2009); Scoular & Linley (2006); Sparrow (2008); Stewart, Palmer, Wilkin, & Kerrin (2008); Ting & Hart (2003); Wycherley & Cox (2008)

Coach & Client Characteristics
Ahern (2005)
Alvey & Barclay (2007)
Axelrod (2005)
Barner & Higgins (2007)
Blackman (2006)
Blukert(2005b)
Bono, Purvanova, Towler, & Peterson (2009)
Dean & Meyer (2002)
Garman, Whiston, & Zlatoper (2000)
Hall, Otazo, & Hollenbeck (1999)
Hollenbeck (2002)
Homan & Miller (2008)
Hooijberg & Lane (2009)
Latham (2007)
Lijenstrand & Nebeker (2008)
Passmore, Rawle-Cope, Gibbes, & Holloway (2006)
Renner (2007)
Stevens (2005)
Stewart, Palmer, Wilkins, & Kerrin (2008)
Sue-Chan & Latham (2004)
Ting & Hart (2003)

Overview
Blukert (2005b); Coutu & Kauffman (2009); Dagley (2006); Dean & Meyer (2002); Feldman & Lankau (2005); Hernez-Broome & Hughes (2004); Hollenbeck (2002); Jay (2003); Joo (2005); Kampa-Kokesch & Anderson (2001); Latham (2007); Lowman (2005); McKenna & Davis (2009); Orenstein (2002); Passmore & Gibbes (2007); Stern (2004); Ting & Hart (2003); Wasylyshyn (2003)

Instead, articles selected for inclusion highlight and reflect the literature in terms of key topics and their relative contributions. Further, the framework and example articles provide a mechanism to examine future literature.

Section 5. Emerging Article Themes

The eighty-one selected articles were coded, outlined, and reviewed. Several themes emerged and are summarized in this section following the Leadership Coaching Framework. Prior to discussing these themes, the coding scheme and outline structure employed with each article is shared. These outlines are located in Section 6.

Each article was coded on several dimensions. In addition to coding the Leadership Coaching Framework categories addressed in the article, each publication was coded on the general nature of the article (for example, conceptual or empirical). Articles with a strong and comprehensive introduction on the topic, as well as those that used a particularly effective methodology in investigating a research question, were designated accordingly. Lastly, each article was coded with the number of references included in the article and the total page length. A full description of the article coding process is provided in Table 1 (p. 4). Overall summaries of the articles collectively included in each category of the Leadership Coaching Framework are presented below.

Overview

The *overview* articles provide a broad appreciation of the current coaching literature and a common ground for interpreting the articles that focus on specific aspects of leadership coaching. This summary draws on a variety of literatures—including training, consulting, industrial and organizational psychology, and human resource practices—to present an overview of trends and issues in executive coaching. The overview includes seven conceptual articles, four literature reviews, two empirical studies, and one viewpoint piece. In reviewing these articles, several distinct issues emerged.

First, executive coaching should be distinguished from mentoring, therapy, and counseling (Feldman & Lankau, 2005; Hollenbeck, 2002; Kampa-Kokesch & Anderson, 2001; Passmore & Gibbes, 2007; Stern, 2004). Although these practices may inform the coaching field (for example, McKenna & Davis, 2009), executive coaching is a distinct form of learning and development that utilizes data gathering, constructive feedback, and a dyadic working relationship to improve the effectiveness of higher-level employees (Feldman & Lankau, 2005; Hollenbeck, 2002; Lowman, 2005; Passmore & Gibbes, 2007).

Articles in the overview section, as well as many throughout the entire sourcebook, also contribute to an understanding of executive coaching by identifying the specific inputs and processes associated with effective executive coaching (Joo, 2005; Ting & Hart, 2003; Passmore & Gibbes, 2007). These aspects of coaching include coach competencies (Bluckert, 2005b; Dean & Meyer, 2002; Stern, 2004; Wasylyshyn, 2003), the need for executive coaching training (Bluckert, 2005b; Dean & Meyer, 2002), and the importance of coach and client fit (Hollenbeck, 2002; Joo, 2005; Ting & Hart, 2003). Effective executive coaching also requires a multilevel approach, in which a coach addresses the specific needs of the executive as well as how that individual relates to the overall system or organization (Orenstein, 2002; Stern, 2004).

These articles also highlight future directions for executive coaching research. A consistent appeal is for the field to develop a common definition of executive coaching that is accepted by both the scientific and applied communities (Kampa-Kokesch & Anderson, 2001; Lowman, 2005; Stern, 2004). These articles argue that the definition should emphasize the unique contribution provided by executive coaching relative to advising, mentoring, therapy, and counseling. In addition, more empirical research should be conducted to validate currently recommended practices as well as identify potential moderators (for example, individual differences, measurements, and contexts) of the executive coaching processes (Kampa-Kokesch & Anderson, 2001; Passmore & Gibbes, 2007).

Coach and Client Characteristics

Coach and client characteristics articles address coach and client attributes that are potentially critical to the coaching process. Identifying coach characteristics—including knowledge, skills, and abilities that are essential for effective coaching—and potential clients who will benefit from coaching is critical for understanding how the individuals involved influence coaching outcomes and who should be involved in the coaching process itself. Relevant coach variables likely include coaching philosophy, coaching competencies, and experience, motivation, and personality attributes. Relevant client variables include readiness, skill needs, developmental goals, prior coaching experience, motivation, and personality attributes.

Pre-coaching activities involve conducting a needs-and-readiness assessment to select coaches who possess the requisite skills and abilities and to identify clients who are receptive and prepared for coaching; this is done to increase the probability of successful coaching outcomes. Determining resources required for executive coaching, and the manner in which organizations select coaches (Hollenbeck, 2002) and clients to receive coaching, have received a relatively high degree of attention (Ting & Hart, 2003).

Many of these articles investigate coach characteristics deemed important by clients and experienced coaches (Blackman, 2006; Hall, Otazo, & Hollenbeck, 1999). Characteristics identified as important include good communication and listening skills, credibility and experience, integrity, empathy, intelligence, psychological mindedness, assessment knowledge, motivational skills, ability to develop rapport, and business knowledge (Blackman, 2006; Blukert 2005b; Dean & Meyer, 2002; Hall et al., 1999; Stevens, 2005).

Many articles also compare the effectiveness or perceived effectiveness of coaches based on who provides the coaching, such as an internal or external coach (Ahern, 2005; Hall et al., 1999; Sue-Chan & Latham, 2004), or on the educational background of the coach (Barner & Higgins, 2007; Bono, Purvanova, Towler, & Peterson, 2009; Garman, Whiston, & Zlatoper, 2000; Homan & Miller, 2008; Liljenstrand & Nebeker, 2008). Overall, there appears to be relatively small differences in coaching as a result of educational background, though psychologists generally are recognized as having a stronger background in measurement and are more likely to use empirically validated techniques (Bono et al., 2009).

The literature on essential client characteristics is less extensive, but characteristics suggested as important for successful coaching to occur include individual readiness, psychological readiness, and environmental readiness (Ting & Hart, 2003), as well as individual difference attributes such as conscientiousness, openness to experience, emotional stability, and general self-efficacy (Stewart, Palmer, Wilkin, & Kerrin, 2008). A related and interesting theme is adapting coaching interventions to meet individual needs, such as the adult development stage of the client (Axelrod, 2005) or clients in less-developed countries (Renner, 2007). Articles of this nature highlight that client characteristics are important not just for identifying potential clients but also for understanding how client characteristics can influence the coaching process itself.

Collectively, these articles provide a foundation for identifying coach and client attributes that are important to consider in the coaching process; however, there are several fruitful and critical areas for future research. First, although a wide variety of coach and client attributes have been identified, many of these articles are conceptual in nature. Empirical research is needed to evaluate the influence of these characteristics on coaching processes and outcomes. Second, a theoretical rationale for why and when attributes of the coach and client matter needs to be considered. For instance, Alvey and Barclay (2007) addressed coach characteristics important for establishing trusting relationships with clients, thus addressing the question of why coach

and client attributes they identified are important. Third, rather than focusing on how educational background influences the coaching process, future
research needs to focus on training that can improve the effectiveness of
coaching (Bono et al., 2009). Finally, focused attention is needed on selection
criteria to determine potential clients most likely to benefit from coaching
and how the coaching engagement may need to change based on the unique
characteristics of individual clients.

Coach-Client Match

Coach-client match is the process of pairing a coach to an individual
client. Although a good match or fit between a client and coach is generally
considered critical to the development of an effective coaching relationship,
consensus regarding which factors are most important and their optimum
composition, as well as effective processes in performing the match, is more
elusive. The Leadership Coaching Framework suggests that the quality of the
coach-client match moderates the effects of coach and client characteristics
on the coaching process and relationship. Based on this literature, coach and
client characteristics that may be relevant in pairing include commonalities
in demographic, professional, and personal backgrounds, compatibility in
behavioral preferences such as personality and work styles, and the coach's
credibility based on his or her competence and experience relative to the client's coaching needs.

The *coach-client match* articles examine the issues related to the matching process as well as the interaction between the characteristics that each
individual brings to the coaching experience. However, the topic is generally
treated as a fringe issue. Twelve of the seventeen articles marginally examine matching within the context of other leadership coaching issues—predominantly coach and client characteristics and coaching process. However,
despite the peripheral attention, five of these articles (Boyce et al., 2010;
Hollenbeck, 2002; Homan & Miller, 2008; O'Broin & Palmer, 2006;
Passmore et al., 2006) provide relatively greater insights on matching issues.
Further, coach-client issues are central to four of the most recent publications (Carr, 2008; Scoular & Linley, 2006; Sparrow, 2008; Wycherley & Cox,
2008), indicative of the emergent interest in supporting the dyadic relationship.

A review of the coach-client-match articles identified three trends
reflecting the state of the literature, the current conceptual and research foci,
and the direction for future research. Unlike the leadership coaching literature
in general, the published articles collected largely examine matching issues
from a research perspective, with seven of the seventeen classified as research

articles. Although the conceptual articles discuss the current matching *processes*, the research articles study the matching *factors*, including compatibility and credibility variables in building client-coach relationships. Most of the articles, however, explicate the need for further research to understand and guide practice, suggesting that any directions or conclusions would be premature. As a whole, these articles contribute to the understanding of matching issues by building on mentoring and psychotherapy literature and laying a foundation on which to build future research. As the research designs employed were often qualitative and less stringent, future research needs to be quantitative, systematic, and rigorous. Employing validated measures, reporting study design details and statistical outcomes, and grounding the work in theory will support the generalizability of the matching results across coaching programs.

Organizational Support

Executive coaching is a form of leadership development that occurs in the context of the workplace (Hernez-Broome & Hughes, 2004) and benefits not only the individual clients receiving coaching but also the organizations they work in (Blackman, 2006; Kampa-Kokesch & Anderson, 2001). Because coaching occurs in the context of an organization, organizational factors are important influences on the executive coaching process (Joo, 2005).

The *organizational support* articles address factors associated with the organizational context in which coaching occurs that impact executive coaching. Many of these articles discuss the direct role that organizations play in selecting coachees as well as determining the coaching goals (Hollenbeck, 2002; Wycherley, 2008). Although coaching in the past was largely provided as a means to "fix" broken employees, organizations are increasingly using coaching as a means of investing in the future of the individual client and organization (Frisch, 2001). Thus, in addition to guiding the goals of coaching, organizations play an important role in how coaching is perceived and in the likelihood that a stigma will be attached to coaching, which can reduce motivation to make the most of the coaching experience.

Support, a component of the assessment, challenge, and support framework, can be provided directly by the organization. A supportive and safe, but challenging, organizational setting and culture positively influences the executive coaching process (Alvey & Barclay, 2007; Ting & Hart, 2003). Additionally, clients' perceptions of supervisory support and motivation to transfer knowledge and skills learned in coaching back to the job have both been observed to be positively related to the coach-client working relationship

(Baron & Morin, 2009). Given the importance observed of organizational support on executive coaching, it is noteworthy that organizations are generally perceived as supportive of the coaching process (Blackman, 2006).

The last issue frequently discussed in these articles highlights the nature of how the organizational context influences the relationship between client and coach. Many of the articles address the influence of the organizational context on trust. Trust is expected to facilitate higher levels of honesty and a willingness to be forthcoming with a coach (Alvey & Barclay, 2007). The organizational context and confidentiality have been observed to be important predictors of trust (Alvey & Barclay, 2007; Gyllensten & Palmer, 2007). Although internal coaches are recognized as possessing an in-depth knowledge of the organization, there is often fear that they may have a conflict of interest between the client and the organization (Hall, Otazo, & Hollenbeck, 1999). External coaches are valued for the stricter confidentiality they may provide, allowing clients to say the "unspeakable" (Hall et al., 1999; Stevens, 2005).

Collectively, the articles addressing the organizational context provide a foundation for understanding the importance of organizational factors on the executive coaching process and outcomes. The consensus appears to be that organizations have a significant influence on coaching processes and outcomes (Hollenbeck, 2002) and that the success of executive coaching depends on understanding the individual client as part of a larger organization (Orenstein, 2002; Tobias, 1996).

None of the articles in this section identify exactly how organizations can provide support as part of the executive coaching process. The discussions generally focus on the organization identifying the best executives to receive coaching and helping to match them with an appropriate coach (Hollenbeck, 2002), or on the value of organizational support (Alvey & Barclay, 2007). The exact role of the organizational system has been identified as one issue in need of greater attention (Orenstein, 2002), with future research needed to identify and understand the specific organizational factors that influence effective executive coaching. Although these articles suggest that this topic is important, it has not received nearly the amount of attention as the other Leadership Coaching Framework components have.

Coaching Process

The coaching process is the core of the coaching engagement and is where the actual act of coaching occurs. As depicted in the Leadership Coaching Framework, the coaching process is partitioned into the logistics of the coaching session, program content or elements, the relationship, and tools and techniques. A review of the articles identified three trends reflecting the state of the literature, the current conceptual and research foci, and the direction for future research.

The vast majority of writing about the coaching process relies heavily on the "practiced wisdom" of seasoned coaches sharing their thoughts, expertise, and experience. The majority of the articles included are conceptual, with only two being research based (Blackman, 2006; Bono et al., 2009). The articles also represent a variety of discipline-related approaches that are used in the coaching process. As more clinical and counseling psychologists enter the arena of executive coaching, they bring with them their training in psychotherapy and theoretical approaches to behavior change. The most common of these are psychoanalytic, humanistic, cognitive-behavioral, and rational emotive (Barner & Higgins, 2007; Cociver & Cronshaw, 2004; Ducharme, 2004; Kilburg, 2004; Passmore, 2007; Sherin & Caiger, 2004).

Although a multitude of ideas and perspectives are offered regarding the critical variables comprising the coaching process, the coaches' theoretical orientation and the application of psychotherapies to the practice of executive coaching are most consistently discussed. Many of the conceptual articles also focus on coach characteristics as an aspect of the process, such as coaches' theoretical orientation, credentialing, and professional experience (note that the Leadership Coaching Framework identifies these as input variables to the process rather than components of the process). The research articles also tend to focus on how coach characteristics such as professional experience and background influence coaching behaviors and thus the coaching process (Blackman, 2006; Bono et al., 2009). The fact that these articles merge and intermingle discussions of input and process variables, as identified by the Leadership Coaching Framework, attests to the complexity of conducting coaching research and identifying the discrete factors that influence coaching.

Also worth noting is that these articles do not map precisely onto the areas identified in the coaching process component of the Leadership Coaching Framework (mechanics, program content, relationship, and tools and techniques). As noted earlier, the majority of articles in this section are theoretical in nature and so do not reflect more concrete variables such as the logistics of the coaching session, assessments, contracting issues, and specific tools and techniques used. To some extent, the articles that focus on the theoretical orientation of the coach touch on the relationship aspect of the process as well as the general techniques used.

All of the articles emphasize the need for further research in order to understand and guide practice. As a whole, these articles contribute to the understanding of the coaching process by building on psychotherapy literature. Future research needs to examine the applicability and generalizability of related fields' research to coaching and validate the importance of process variables' impact on coaching effectiveness.

Medium

An important component of the executive coaching process is the medium through which coaching sessions are conducted. Executive coaches can use a variety of methods to connect and communicate with their clients. Although traditional coaching sessions have often been conducted face to face, increasing technological advances allow the use of other mediums such as teleconferencing, e-mailing, instant messaging, and even virtual simulations.

The *medium* articles address or examine means of coaching other than the traditional face-to-face interactions. Much of the literature consists of conceptual models or anecdotal evidence, with very little empirical research. Nevertheless, extant practices and theoretical models suggest that the coaching environment and medium are important moderators of the executive coaching process. Specifically, face-to-face, technology-supported, or even blended coaching (a combination of technology-mediated and face-to-face coaching) may differentially influence executive coaching outcomes.

In addition, these articles suggest two important themes. First, technology-mediated coaching presents unique benefits and challenges (Driscoll, 2005; Goldsmith, 2006; Pulley, 2006). For example, technology facilitates global communication, as it is more time- and cost-efficient than travel (Driscoll, 2005; Hakim, 2003). In doing so, electronic coaching allows for improved accessibility to coaches by clients (Driscoll, 2005; Goldsmith, 2006; Hamilton & Scandura, 2003; Knouse, 2001). Electronic coaching (e-coaching) also poses challenges. The lack of face-to-face interactions can inhibit quality interpersonal relationships between coach and client (Boyce & Hernez-Broome, 2010; Driscoll, 2005; Mallen et al., 2003). Additionally, coaching technologies may be difficult to use for some individuals (Driscoll, 2005; Goldsmith, 2006), and the constant connectivity can become overwhelming for both coach and client (Goldsmith, 2006).

A second emerging theme emphasizes that different (or perhaps more pronounced) skills may be required of an executive coach, depending on the coaching medium (Boyce & Hernez-Broome, 2010; Goldsmith, 2006;

Hamilton & Scandura, 2003). For example, executive coaches in a virtual environment may need enhanced interpersonal skills in order to overcome the impersonal nature of electronic communication methods (Boyce & Hernez-Broome, 2010; Driscoll, 2005; Mallen, Day, & Green, 2003).

Although limited in number, existing work on e-coaching research lays the foundation for future research efforts. In addition to verifying the similarities and differences between electronic and traditional coaching, research should examine the differences among e-coaching methods (for example, telephone, e-mail, teleconferencing, and avatars). Additional research is also needed on the practice of blended coaching and how it can be successfully implemented (Pulley, 2006). Continuing this research will provide a greater understanding of the specific dynamics created by e-coaching mediums, and ultimately a wider repertoire of empirically sound e-coaching practices.

Coaching Outcomes

Despite the rising popularity of leadership coaching, the scarcity of evaluations of coaching engagements has been a systematic complaint within the coaching literature (Feldman & Lankau, 2005; Joo, 2005). The *coaching outcomes* articles focus on measuring coaching impact in order to evaluate coaching engagements. Identifying and measuring appropriate coaching outcomes is critical for studying the coaching process and providing a foundation for understanding the factors that contribute to successful coaching engagements. These articles highlight the different methodologies used and outcomes examined in coaching evaluation research.

In general, coaching studies have been criticized for their lack of methodological rigor (for example, Feldman & Lankau, 2005). Although some of the studies included in our review suffered from methodological limitations such as small sample sizes (for example, Jones et al., 2006; Levenson, 2009; Orenstein, 2006), several of the studies exhibited rigorous methodologies such as using experimental designs—examining client changes from pre- to post-coaching and/or comparing outcomes against a control condition (for example, Evers et al., 2006; Smither et al., 2003) and incorporating multisource data (e.g., Smither et al., 2003; Thach, 2002).

Studies examining coaching outcomes have also moved beyond simple assessments of clients' satisfaction with coaching. A range of criteria are being explored, including self-efficacy (Baron & Morin, 2010; Evers, Brouwers, & Tomic, 2006), flexibility (Jones, Rafferty, & Griffin, 2006), and leadership behaviors or performance (De Meuse et al., 2009; Orenstein, 2006; Smither, London, Flautt, Vargas, & Kucine, 2003).

Although progress has been made in the evaluation of coaching engagements, there are several directions where future research is needed to bring added validity to the coaching evaluation literature. First, the nature of leadership as social influence calls for a multilevel perspective of coaching outcomes that include changes in the attitudes, performance, and retention of both the client and the client's subordinates. Second, research evaluating coaching engagements should include a focus on distal outcomes. Some of the most valuable organizational outcomes (for example, leadership retention and an adequate pipeline to fill senior positions) may not be observable until months or years after the coaching intervention has ended. As coaching continues to mature as an approach to leadership development, we anticipate that evaluation approaches will also continue to mature as researchers and practitioners work together to evaluate coaching outcomes.

Conclusion

The Leadership Coaching Sourcebook presents the most current and solid research on executive coaching. The articles represent a multitude of ideas and perspectives regarding the factors and specific variables critical to coaching, which may be a reflection of the complexity and individualistic nature of coaching engagements. Further, despite the relatively narrow time band, with most articles published in the past decade, the evolution of the field is evident in terms of theoretical discussions and empirical research.

Consistent with this growth is the constant request for more empirical research in almost every aspect of the field, from the most fundamental level of developing a common definition of coaching to research that explores virtual coaching. This message is also reflected in the nature of the articles included in this sourcebook. Despite our efforts to seek out empirically based research, most of the articles presented are theoretical in nature or are based on the experience of the respective authors.

The good news is that although limited, the existing empirical research affirms the effectiveness and value of executive coaching (Dagley, 2006; Kampa-Kokesch & Anderson, 2001; Passmore & Gibbes, 2007). Furthermore, research is becoming more systematic and is identifying and investigating the specific inputs, processes, and outcomes associated with executive coaching (Joo, 2005; Passmore & Gibbes, 2007; Ting & Hart, 2003). In addition, with regard to the evaluation of coaching, more rigorous studies are being conducted, adopting experimental designs that examine client changes from pre- to post-coaching and/or comparing outcomes against a control condition (for example, Evers et al., 2006; Smither et al., 2003).

Although the quantity and quality of research on coaching is improving, much work remains to be done. However, we are confident that as researchers and practitioners alike begin to think about coaching in a more systematic manner, the rigor of the research will improve and many of the current gaps in our knowledge will be addressed. This sourcebook provides a strong contribution to move us in that direction. The intent of the sourcebook is to organize the most current coaching literature cohesively and systematically and in doing so to provide a bearing for the current state of coaching research, including where there is a concentration of effort and where gaps exist. We acknowledge that the literature represented in this sourcebook is not exhaustive. As noted previously, our intent was to keep the sourcebook manageable, so we focused our selection of publications for each section. Thus it is possible that worthwhile publications on executive coaching have not been included, but we believe we have represented the limited empirical research.

We encourage practitioners and researchers alike to incorporate the best available knowledge from research, theory, and practice with their expertise to inform the practice of coaching, and hope that informed practice will in turn generate and stimulate excitement for more opportunities to conduct rigorous empirical research.

Section 6. Article Outlines

Ahern, G. (2005). Coaching professionalism and provider size. *Journal of Management Development, 24*(1)**, 94–99.**

Relevant Sections: Coach and Client Characteristics

Purpose
- Essay on professional qualities of externally supplied coaches

Design / Methodology
- Examination of three provider size-types in relation to characteristic quality issues
  - Large conglomerates (often multinational)
  - Solo market (coaches work as individuals)
  - "Boutique" specialized coaching teams
- Characteristics Quality Variables
  - Clear initial framing (e.g., distinguishing coaching from consulting)
  - Written and distributed guidelines
  - Separating coaching project management from its delivery
  - Capability to match individual clients to appropriate coaches
  - External qualified supervision
  - Formal evaluation and internal quality control
  - Achieved confidentiality
  - Data protection
  - Securing a professional coaching identity

Findings / Implications
- Professional quality characteristically varies with different types of coaching provider
- Suggests provider size is key quality-related variable by offering pros and cons for each

Originality / Value
- Considers provider size as a key variable in coach quality

Strengths
- Provides examples to illustrate arguments

Limitations
- Discussion based only on author's subjective field experience

Categories: T5, C1, P6

***

Alvey, S., & Barclay, K. (2007). The characteristics of dyadic trust in executive coaching. *Journal of Leadership Studies, 1*(1), 18–27.

Relevant Sections: Coaching Process, Coach and Client Characteristics, Organizational Support, Coach-Client Matching

Purpose
- Explore development of trust in executive coaching relationships

Design / Methodology
- Semi-structured 35- to 45-minute phone interviews with high-level executives
  - 14 of 80 coaches contacted recommended 32 executives; 27 participated
  - 14 male/13 female; 30–50 years old, high-level executives (e.g., VP, GM)
  - Content analyzed using Atlas.ti; used 81 codes developed during manual analysis
  - Interrater reliability assessed by two raters with five transcripts (IRR not reported)
- Interviews coded for client readiness, organizational support, and coach behavioral styles

Findings / Implications
- Interplay of relational, situational, and behavioral factors influence development of trust
- Characteristics of close and trusting coaching relationship
  - Client readiness: willingness to change, willingness to disclose, open to feedback
  - Higher levels of honesty and willingness to be forthcoming with coaches
- Coaching situation setting the context for trust
  - Confidentiality was the single most important factor in developing/maintaining trust
  - Organizational Context: Organizational support and positive culture
  - Articulation of goals and approach (ground rules) helps define relationship
  - Use of assessment tools early in the relationship
  - Coaching Outcomes: professional advancement; balance professional/personal
- Coach characteristics and behaviors for establishing trusting relationships

- o Coach credibility: experience in business and experience as a coach
- o Coach background initially important; coach behaviors more important later
- o Coach's objectivity/neutrality; supportive, confirming, and challenging behaviors
- Low Factors of Trust Development
  - o Payment arrangements had no significant impact on trust or satisfaction
  - o Gender, Location/Forum, Coaching Frequency, Coaching Certification

Originality / Value

- Presents five factors contributing to the development of trust as perceived by the client
  1. Contextual (client readiness, organizational support)
  2. Introductory (coach credibility)
  3. Agreement (articulation of goals/approach, confidentiality)
  4. Behavioral (Confirming → Challenging)
  5. Outcome (perception of values, outcome of goals)

Strengths

- Provides interview quotes to illustrate findings
- Figure 1 summarizes essential factors of trust development (positive and negative)
- Figure 2 presents model of chronological factors contributing to trust development

Limitations

- No information regarding subject selection qualifications criteria
- No evidence for claims of significance
- Trust differences between clients nominated by coaches and non-nominated clients

Categories: T2, C36, P9

✳ ✳ ✳

Armstrong, H. B., Melser, P. J., & Tooth, J. A. (2007). Executive coaching effectiveness: A pathway to self-efficacy. Sydney: Institute of Executive Coaching. Retrieved November 16, 2008, from http://www.iecoaching.com/files/CES%20Results%20Full%20Version%2003%2007.pdf

Relevant Sections: Coaching Process, Coach-Client Matching, Coaching Outcomes

Purpose
- Evaluate coaching effectiveness to improve coaching approach and practice
- Develop benchmarks for coaching effectiveness
- Understand benefits of coaching from client perspective

Design / Methodology
- Benchmarking study using a 15-minute online survey and semi-structured interviews
- 111 clients completed survey; 30 random clients interviewed
- Overall measure of client satisfaction and subjective assessments of benefit
- Measure of effectiveness of achieving changes/goals coaching expected to address
- Measure of client readiness based on client expectations and attitudes
- Measure of coaching relationship qualities that contribute to effectiveness

Findings / Implications
- Positive relationship between importance of an outcome and extent outcome achieved
- Benefits categorized by Self, Team, Organization, Career Direction, Work Life Adjustment (task performance and aspects of work life); reported using percentage responding
    - Benefits rated most high related to self-perception and impact on workplace relationships; suggests coaching impacts intra- and interpersonal relationships
    - Pursuing career goals and setting direction for self and others also rated high
- Ratings of coaching factors contributing to coaching effectiveness
    - Factors promoting meaningful personal and private conversations rated higher in importance
    - Factors emphasizing conventional learning, skill development or help with work organization rated lower in importance

Originality / Value

- Provides global perspective with qualitative insights regarding perceived benefits of coaching beyond Kirkpatrick's framework; also considers coaching relationships

Strengths

- Presents coaching framework that integrates qualities of coaching relationship
- Discusses training evaluation in terms of the relationship process (e.g., characteristics of the relationship account for 30 percent of effectiveness)
- Shares qualitative data with examples of written comments

Limitations

- Focuses only on the IEC coaching framework with minimal discussion to support
- Includes references to other research and relevant literature, though not succinctly
- Details of survey items not provided, although examples of items are found in tables
- Information regarding the survey and interview population/sample not presented
- Did not perform statistical analysis, comparison based on percentage of respondents and by item

Categories: T2, C53, P30

✳ ✳ ✳

Axelrod, S. D. (2005). Executive growth along the adult development curve. *Consulting Psychology Journal: Practice and Research, 57,* **118–125.**

Relevant Sections: Coach and Client Characteristics

Purpose

- Discuss relevance of principles of adult psychological development to executive coaching

Design / Methodology

- Conceptual article that uses an adult developmental perspective to identify key transformational tasks of adulthood that help shape executive role functioning
- Case studies provide examples of key points

Findings / Implications

- Argues that core issues of adult development can serve as a template for evaluating executive competencies and fostering personal and professional growth
    - Adult development and growth of psychological and leadership competencies argued to help aid emerging capabilities contributing to job performance and personal growth
- Argues that interventions for behavioral change will be most effective when they are based on an understanding of where the client is on adult development curve
    - Middle managers are often at midlife
        - Lots of drive and ambition but require more interpersonal skills
    - Executive vice presidents are often at late midlife
        - Issues of continuing commitment to work and organizational life need attention
- Argues that coaches need to be mindful of what a client is trying to accomplish as both a leader and more broadly as an individual

Originality / Value

- Examines implications of adult development for the executive coaching process

Strengths

- Provides foundation for understanding developmental needs of coaches

Limitations

- Empirical support needed for framework

Categories: T4, C14, P8

✳ ✳ ✳

Barner, R., & Higgins, J. (2007). Understanding implicit models that guide the coaching process. *Journal of Management Development,* *26*(2), 148–158.

Relevant Sections: Coaching Process, Coach and Client Characteristics

Purpose

- Present four prevailing theory-based models that inform coaching practice
- Discuss how the theoretical approach adopted shapes one's coaching practice

Design / Methodology
- Based on authors' combined 30 years of experience
- Organizational examples illustrate key concepts

Findings / Implications
- Coaches are eclectic in the methods they use but tend to center their practice around one of the four coaching models
    - Clinical model helps client gain insight into himself or herself as a leader to effect constructive changes in performance
    - Behavioral model supports personal change by encouraging clients to understand the impact of their behavior on themselves and others
    - Systems model emphasizes understanding the organizational context in which client behavior is embedded
    - Social constructionist model contends that it is through social interactions and symbolic frameworks that social identities are created
- These models inform the practice and shape the approaches coaches take in choosing their assessments and interventions
- Thinking through their theoretical assumptions, limitations, and caveats of models used allows coaches to bring a higher level of discipline and effectiveness into the coaching process and ensures client expectations are met

Originality / Value
- Serves as a think piece for coaches
- Encourages coaches to reflect on how each individual's practice is developed from, and informed by, a particular theory position
- Applies the four models to a hypothetical coaching situation

Strengths
- Bridges theory and practice
- Includes tables that provide a good summary of key characteristics that differentiate the four models, including:
    - Goals of coaching
    - Where the change occurs
    - View of the coach's role
    - Focus of the coaching

Limitations
- Is not comprehensive in delineating the differences among the four models
- Only touches on the conditions that may determine which approach should be used

Categories: T1, C34, P9

* * *

Baron, L., & Morin, L. (2009). The coach-coachee relationship in executive coaching: A field study. *Human Resource Development Quarterly, 20*(1), 85–106.

Relevant Sections: Coaching Process, Coach-Client Matching, Organizational Support

Purpose

- Investigate role of coach-client relationship in increasing client self-efficacy

Design / Methodology

- Field study conducted at a large North American manufacturing company
- Survey data collected from 31 coaching dyads (58 percent client, 38 percent coach response rates)
  - 73 managers (average age 38 with 4.7 years experience as managers); 24 "certified" coaches
  - Data collected on Day One of eight-day classroom seminar and five months later
  - Executive coaching consisted of up to 14 90-minute face-to-face sessions
- *Client Self-Efficacy*: 8 items, 11-point Likert-type scale developed for the study
- *Coach-Client Working Relationship*: 12 items, 7-point Likert scale from Working Alliance Inventory (WAI-S short form; Corbiere et al., 2006; Tracey & Kokotovic, 1989)
- *Executive Coaching*: number of coaching sessions
- *Coach's Self-Efficacy*: 18 items, 11-point Likert scale developed for the study; conceptual groupings were *relational skills* (a = .75), *communication skills* (a = .60), *ability to facilitate learning and results* (a = .76; appendix includes all items)
- *Motivation to Transfer*: 4 items, 5-point Likert scale from Learning Transfer System Inventory (LTSI; Holton, Bates, & Ruona, 2000)
- *Supervisor Support*: 6 items from LTSI

Findings / Implications

- Coach-client relationship mediates coaching sessions and client's post self-efficacy
- Four (of six) variables significantly correlated with Coach-Client Working Relationship

- o Coach's facilitating learning and results self-efficacy ($r = .42$, $p < .01$)
- o Client's motivation to transfer ($r = .36, p < .01$)
- o Client's perception of supervisor support ($r = .29, p < .05$)
- o Number of coaching sessions ($r = .32, p < .01$)
- o Two nonsignificant variables: coaching skills (relational, communication)

Originality / Value
- Provides support that coach-client relationship is a prerequisite for coaching effectiveness
- Discusses and encourages research regarding the interpersonal fit between the coach and client and issues of organizational culture and support

Strengths
- Focuses on the coach-client relationship; informed by psychotherapy literature
- Summarizes the current relevant literature, including a discussion of three empirical coach-client relationship studies (Berry, 2005; Dingman, 2004; McGovern et al., 2001)

Limitations
- Coach self-efficacy categories are conceptually based with low item reliabilities

Categories: T2, I, M, C77, P21

∗ ∗ ∗

Baron, L., & Morin, L. (2010). The impact of executive coaching on self-efficacy related to management soft-skills. *Leadership & Organization Development Journal, 31*(1), 18–38.

Relevant Sections: Coaching Outcomes

Purpose
- Examine the effects of coaching on junior and mid-level managers' efficacy for engaging in leadership behaviors

Design / Methodology
- Empirical article that used a pre/post design to examine the effect of coaching on leadership self-efficacy
- Participants included 73 junior and mid-level managers (63 men and 10 women) enrolled in an eight-month leadership development program that included a coaching component

     ○ The number of coaching sessions was left up to the coach and client to decide—the number of sessions ranged from 1 to 11, with an average of 5 sessions
- Self-efficacy was assessed at the beginning of the leadership development program and then again eight months later

Findings / Implications
- In support of their hypothesis, the authors found a positive and significant relationship between the number of coaching sessions a participant went through and their post-coaching self-efficacy ($r = .28$)

Originality / Value
- Highlights the importance of examining criteria such as self-efficacy when evaluating coaching effectiveness

Strengths
- Pre/post design

Limitations
- No measure of the quality of the coaching sessions or what the focus was of the sessions
- Causality of relationship unclear—may have been that a drop in self-efficacy led to fewer coaching sessions

Categories: T2, I, C99, P21

✱ ✱ ✱

Berman, W. H., & Brandt, G. (2006). Executive coaching and consulting: "Different strokes for different folks." *Professional Psychology: Research and Practice, 37*(3), 244–253.

Relevant Sections: Coaching Process

Purpose
- Define and clarify the balance between business and psychological competencies in executive coaching
- Proposes a four-category model of coaching methods:
    1. Facilitative coaching ensures new leaders implement the steps likely to achieve their personal and strategic goals
    2. Executive consulting offers senior leaders a thoughtful, challenging relationship with a neutral third party to think through difficult issues
    3. Restorative coaching helps a valued individual overcome short-term problems at work due to personal or organizational changes

4. Developmental coaching builds strengths and addresses deficits in a mission-critical individual who has substantial and long-standing challenges and interpersonal issues

Design / Methodology

- The two authors' unique conceptualization of executive coaching and consulting based on their highly divergent backgrounds, training, and experience
- Through the course of the authors' collaboration, skills and competencies were differentiated, resulting in systematic and individual methods identified to best help clients

Findings / Implications

- A four-category model of executive coaching is defined by the intersection of focus (business versus personal) and technique (brief-directive versus extended-Socratic), producing four quadrants into which each of the four models fit
- There are many types of executive coaching and consulting but only some relate to traditional mental health services
- The shift of clinical psychologists to the corporate world is reasonable and achievable but requires effort and training or experience in the upper levels of the business world
- Training or experience in the upper levels of the business world is essential to developing the capability to help corporate leaders
- Developmental coaching is the most likely fit with traditional psychological training

Originality / Value

- Provides good insight into the role of psychology in executive coaching
- Presents a practical model of coaching that is straightforward and easily understood

Strengths

- Case examples provided
- Very specific "how to" information regarding the coaching skills required and coach's role for each coaching model
- Nine practical steps are outlined for becoming a successful coach

Limitations: None noted

Categories: T1, C34, P17

* * *

Blackman, A. (2006). Factors that contribute to the effectiveness of business coaching: The coachees' perspective. *The Business Review, Cambridge, 5*, 98–104.

Relevant Sections: Coach and Client Characteristics, Coaching Process, Organizational Support

Purpose
- Examine factors that coachees consider effective in the coaching process

Design / Methodology
- Questionnaires with both quantitative and qualitative questions administered to industry professionals who had been or were currently engaged in executive coaching
  - Questions asked about the coach, coachee, organization, and the coaching process
  - $N = 114$ clients
  - Open-ended questions content analyzed

Findings / Implications
- When asked to rank the importance of the coach, coachee, and what the coach does, participants were most likely to report the coach (35.1 percent) or what the coach does (33.3 percent) as most important
- Features of a coach identified as the most important were good communication skills (13.6 percent), credibility and experience (9.7 percent), empathy (9 percent), knowledge (8 percent), and sufficient contact time (4.7 percent)
- Factors perceived to contribute most to a coach's effectiveness were maintaining confidentiality, communicating clearly, honesty, organization, and displaying self-confidence
- Features of the coaching process identified as most important were identifying blind spots, receiving help to constructively view difficult issues, and being encouraged to take appropriate action
- Most respondents believe their organization was very supportive (41.2 percent) or generally supportive (32.5 percent) of the coaching process
- The most frequently cited goals for participating in coaching were to get a promotion, add value to the organization, improve in one's role, or become more effective
- The majority felt they put a great deal of effort into the coaching process (79.8 percent)
- The biggest barrier in the coaching process identified was preoccupation with work matters (66.7 percent)

Originality / Value
- Examines a variety of factors influencing the coaching process
- Examines executive coaching from the perspective of the coachee

Strengths
- Considers a wide variety of factors influencing the coaching proces

Limitations
- Little background information on sample
- Only self-report data collected

Categories: T2, C21, P7

∗ ∗ ∗

Blukert, P. (2005). Critical factors in executive coaching—the coaching relationship. *Industrial and Commercial Training*, **37(7), 336–340.**

Relevant Sections: Coaching Process

Purpose
- Examine the coaching relationship as a critical success factor in executive coaching
- Outline the characteristics of a successful coaching relationship and how to establish it

Design / Methodology
- Article is based on the basic proposition that the coaching relationship is the critical factor in successful coaching outcomes
- Characteristics of successful coaching relationships are explored

Findings / Implications
- A need to shift the emphasis of coach training more strongly toward the coaching relationship and improving coach with relationship-building skills
- Link is made to client-centered counseling and the influence of "Rogerian" thinking
- Characteristics of a successful coaching relationship include:
    - Client-centered thinking
    - Establishing rapport
    - Support and challenge
    - Trust
- When reflecting on their coaching experience clients remember the coach as a person, not the tools or psychological frameworks used

Originality / Value
- Emphasizes the importance of the coaching relationship as a critical success factor in executive coaching rather than the current literature's more common focus on coaching models and techniques

Strengths
- Focuses on the coaching relationship, which is an underemphasized aspect of the coaching process in current literature
- Highlights importance of coaching relationship

Limitations
- Given the proposed importance of the coaching relationship, the article only begins to skim the surface of its complexity

Categories: T1, C4, P5

∗ ∗ ∗

Bluckert, P. (2005). The foundation of a psychological approach to executive coaching. *Industrial and Commercial Training, 37(4),* 171–178.

Relevant Sections: Overview, Coach-Coachee Characteristics

Purpose
- Examine concept of psychological mindedness as an important yet neglected foundation for executive coaching

Design / Methodology
- Defines coaching and psychological mindedness
- Outlines ways to develop psychological mindedness
- Explores the training and development of executive coaches

Findings / Implications
- Psychological mindedness is critical for the personal development of the coach as well as the development of a sound coach-coachee relationship
- Psychological mindedness requires both self- and other-awareness on the part of the executive coach
- Executive coaches can be taught the skills necessary for developing psychological mindedness
  - These skills include asking probing questions, becoming more observant, recognizing behavior patterns, and forming meaningful connections with the environment

Originality / Value
- Very little of the executive coaching literature addresses the importance of psychological mindedness in coaching training and practices

Strengths
- Provides several definitions of executive coaching
- Outlines why psychological mindedness is important, as well as ways in which to develop psychological mindedness

Limitations
- No validation of the author's Coach Competency Inventory (CCI), or process of developing psychological mindedness

Categories: T1, I, C14, P8

✳ ✳ ✳

Bono, J. E., Purvanova, R. K., Towler, A. J., & Peterson, D. B. (2009). A survey of executive coaching practices. *Personnel Psychology*, *62*(2), 361–404.

Relevant Sections: Coaching Process, Coach and Client Characteristics

Purpose
- Address the role of psychology in executive coaching
- Compare the practices of psychologist and nonpsychologist coaches as well as the practices of coaches from various psychological disciplines

Design / Methodology
- 428 coaches (256 nonpsychologists, 172 psychologists)
- Web-based survey was administered
- Dependent variables:
  - Coaching practices
  - Coaching outcomes
  - Coach competencies

Findings / Implications
- Differences in coaching practices between psychologists and nonpsychologists were small (average $d = .26$)
- There were as many differences between psychologists from varying disciplines as there were between psychologists and nonpsychologists
- Caution against relying on educational background to predict a coach's philosophy, process, or behavior
- Need to focus on training that will help all coaches be more effective

- As a whole results appear to favor psychologist coaches, especially
  with respect to strong measurement, use of data from multiple sources,
  and use of techniques with empirical validity

Originality / Value
- Provides a broad snapshot of the field of executive coaching
- Provides evidence that suggests the field of executive coaching should
  move beyond questioning the importance of psychological training for
  executive coaches to more pressing and relevant issues such as:
  - o The knowledge, skills, and abilities coaches need to help clients
    gain insight and motivation
  - o Coach behaviors that are the best predictors of long-term
    behavior change

Strengths
- A large representative sample of coaches with a variety of backgrounds
  and institutional affiliations was used

Limitations
- Survey methodology limited the ability to collect rich data on the
  intricacy of coaches' practices
- Coaches self-reported their behaviors and approaches

Categories: T2, I, C52, P43

✳ ✳ ✳

**Boyce, L. A., & Hernez-Broome, G. (2010). E-coaching: Considerations
of leadership coaching in a virtual environment. In D. Clutterbuck
& Z. Hussain (Eds.), *Virtual coach, virtual mentor* (pp. 139–174).
Charlotte, NC: Information Age Publishing.**

Relevant Sections: Coaching Mediums

Purpose
- Outline a framework for executive electronic coaching (e-coaching),
  which includes four major components:
  1. Coach and coachee characteristics
  2. Coach-client match
  3. Coaching process
  4. Coaching outcomes
- Each component is examined in terms of an overview, examples,
  current research findings, as well as concerns and guidance for the
  future

Design / Methodology
- Draws on e-coaching research and anecdotal evidence from coaches, e-coachees, and organizations
- Presents model of coaching inputs, processes, outcomes, and moderators

Findings / Implications
- Important coach and coachee characteristics include readiness, motivation, and experience
  - o While these are useful characteristics in any coaching relationship, their effects may be more pronounced in the complex electronic environment
- Coach-client match is especially important, as virtual avenues pose interpersonal and communicative barriers
  - o Coach's ability to establish commonalities and rapport via electronic means may help mitigate these challenges
- Coaching processes such as building trust and reducing miscommunication should be employed to reduce e-coaching drawbacks
- Assessment of e-coaching outcomes is vital for evaluating, understanding, and improving common practices

Originality / Value
- Employs an I-P-O model to address key issues in e-coaching research

Strengths
- Provides concise and clear framework for understanding e-coaching aspects
- Outlines concrete suggestions for responding to challenges of e-coaching

Limitations
- Does not address limitations of e-coaching or practice of blended coaching
- Many conclusions drawn from anecdotal evidence without scientific backing

Categories: T1, I, M, C65, P34

* * *

Boyce, L. A., Jackson, R. J., & Neal, L. (2010). Building successful leadership coaching relationships: Examining impact of matching criteria in a leadership coaching program. *Journal of Management Development, 29*(10), 914–931.

Relevant Sections: Coach-Client Matching, Coaching Process

Purpose
- Examine the impact of relationship processes on coaching outcomes
- Examine mediating role of coaching relationship between client-coach match criteria and coaching outcomes

Design / Methodology
- Empirical study at a military service academy
  - 74 client-coach pairs randomly or systematically matched
  - Undergraduate clients participating in a leadership coaching program: 65 percent male
  - Leadership coaches: 75 percent male, 86 percent military
- Data collected over two years
  - Pre-survey measures: commonality (bio data such as gender, ethnicity, hobbies), compatibility (Managerial Grid, Learning Style), credibility (leadership competencies ratings, military experience)
  - Post-survey measures: rapport, trust, commitment, outcomes (client and coach reactions, behavioral change, coaching program results), manipulation check
- Coaching program designed to support the development of leadership competencies for current and future leadership roles
  - Average eight face-to-face meetings between 10 and 90 minutes
  - 77 percent communicated biweekly

Findings / Implications
- Relationship process of rapport, trust, and commitment positively predicted coaching outcomes
- Client-coach relationship fully mediated compatibility and credibility match criteria with coaching outcomes

Originality / Value
- Employs conceptual framework to systematically examine client-coach match criteria in terms of understanding their impact on coaching relationships and outcomes

Strengths
- Presents empirical evidence that client-coach relationships are critical to successful coaching and that different aspects of the relationships uniquely impact outcomes

- Provides evidence that complementary styles support the development of relationships

Limitations
- Standard statistics (e.g., means, standard deviations, correlations) not reported
- Figure illustrating the modeling of the coaching relationship not presented
- Limited generalizability

Categories: T2, I, M, C57, P18

✳ ✳ ✳

Carr, R. (2008). Coach referral services: Do they work? *International Journal of Evidence Based Coaching and Mentoring, 6(2), 114–119.*

Relevant Sections: Coach-Client Matching

Purpose
- Examine value of services that match clients and coaches
- Propose three questions regarding the added value of the International Coach Federation's (ICF) coach referral services (CRS)

Design / Methodology
- Query extended to 200 ICF coaches listed in the CRS (60 percent response rate)
- Participants responded by e-mail regarding a question on the value of the ICF CRS

Findings / Implications
- Describes how coach referral services work
    - Improved coach-client match expected to facilitate successful coaching
    - Typically match client preferences and goals with coach qualifications and expertise
- Indicates a large variation in how the match is determined and accomplished
    - Potential clients enter personal data and coach requirements, which generate lists of coaches with descriptions and qualifications
    - Search engine requires selection of keywords or phrases
    - Static list of coaches and their qualifications from which a client selects a coach

- o Referral service interviews prospective client, determines readiness, provides list and details of coaches who meet client's needs
- Indicates that qualification requirements of coaches vary
  - o Minimal with no screening, organization membership, specific requirements
  - o Many coaches listed more than 50 areas of specialty as part of their coaching profile
- Concludes that ICF CRS minimally generates client revenue

Originality / Value
- Presents a logical discussion of the nature of coach referral services
- Hyperlinks to a chart of reputable coach referral and coach/client matching services

Strengths
- Introduction summarizes interesting data on the state of executive coaching
  - o Coaching generates $1.5 billion in revenue worldwide (ICF, 2007)
  - o Estimated 30,000 coaches around the world (Carr, 2005a)
  - o 291 coach training organizations (compared with less than a dozen in 1999)
  - o More than 60 coaching credentials awarded by coaching schools and organizations (Carr, 2005b)
  - o Half-million individual coach Web sites
  - o 12,000 members in ICF, largest membership in coaching industry

Limitations
- No information provided regarding the coach respondents to determine if they were representative coaches
- No statistics provided regarding their responses (e.g., vast majority, most, few)

Categories: T1, C5, P6

* * *

Cocivera, T., & Cronshaw, S. (2004). Action frame theory as a practical framework for the executive coaching process. *Consulting Psychology Journal: Practice and Research, 56*(4), 234–245.

Relevant Sections: Coaching Process

Purpose
- Explain how action frame theory (AFT) can be applied throughout a typical coaching process
- Build on Kilburg's (2000) model of executive coaching

Design / Methodology
- Demonstrates application of AFT in an actual coaching assignment as an analytic tool as well as a framework for planning and reviewing actions and results

Findings / Implications
- Clarifies definitions of each AFT element
    - Conditions: Constraints inherent in the situation over which the client has no direct control and must be considered as givens
    - Means: Enablers within the client's control that can be brought to bear in shaping the action to achieve the result
    - Action: Goal-directed and voluntary movement of the client physically, mentally, and socially toward a desired state
    - Result: A systems state desired or not by the client and wanted or not by the organization
    - Consequence: Normative evaluation of the result and future impact on the client and the organization
- Four phases of the coaching process are mapped onto the foci of AFT
    - Phase 1, *defining job context,* maps to AFT component *identifying conditions*
    - Phase 2, *assessment,* maps to AFT component *determining means*
    - Phase 3, *providing feedback,* maps to AFT components *action* and *results*
    - Phase 4, *implementation and follow-up,* maps to AFT component *consequences*
- By applying AFT in a systematic way, executive coaches can collect behavioral information helpful to the coaching engagement
- AFT provides a broad, holistic view of and approach to coaching engagements that fits with existing coaching models and processes

Originality / Value
- Discusses a very specific and different approach to executive coaching

Strengths
- Steps the reader through what AFT is, how it augments a current model of executive coaching (Kilburg, 2000), and how to apply it
- Provides insight and practical information to coaches as to how to apply AFT to their own coaching process

Limitations: None noted

Categories: T1, C13, P12

✳ ✳ ✳

Coutu, D., & Kauffman, C. (2009). What can coaches do for you?
Harvard Business Review, 87(1), 91–97.

Relevant Sections: Overview

Purpose
- Examine the current state of executive coaching

Design / Methodology
- Survey of 140 coaches with commentary from five experts: Ram Charan, David Peterson, Michael Maccoby, Anne Scoular, Anthony Grant
- Sample: equally men and women
  - 71 percent from the United States; 18 percent from the United Kingdom
  - 61 percent more than 10 years of experience
  - Background: 50 percent business or consulting; 20 percent psychology

Findings / Implications
- Example of survey results highlighted with percentage responding
  - Reasons coaches are engaged: Develop high potentials or facilitate transition (48 percent), address derailing behavior (12 percent)
  - Coaching costs per hour: Range $200 to $3,500; Medium $500
  - Duration: Range 7 to 12 months
  - Necessity of certification: Very 29 percent; Not at all 28 percent
- Expert commentaries suggest
  - The coaching industry will continue to grow, particularly in developing economies (e.g., Brazil, China, India, Russia)
  - The coaching industry is fragmented and needs a leader to define the profession

      o Impact of coaching needs to be demonstrated and measured quantitatively and qualitatively

      o Purpose of coaching is dynamic and evolving and will continue to expand

Originality / Value

- Provides a brief summary of the state of executive coaching

Strengths

- Commentary provides differential insights on the survey results
- Survey is broad, including client characteristics (readiness), matching, and process (coaching tools) issues

Limitations

- Sample was by invitation only (70 percent response rate)
- Complete results of the *Harvard Business Review* survey at HBR Web site no longer available

Categories: T2, C0, P7

✳ ✳ ✳

Dagley, G. (2006). Human resources professionals' perceptions of executive coaching: Efficacy, benefits and return on investment. *International Coaching Psychology Review, 1*, 34–44.

Relevant Sections: Overview, Coaching Outcomes

Purpose

- Survey human resource (HR) professionals on their opinions of executive coaching

Design / Methodology

- Face-to-face, structured interviews
- Sampled Melbourne-based HR professionals from both public and private sectors
- Participants were asked to rate executive coaching practices on a 5-point Likert-type scale

Findings / Implications

- Participants cited executive coaching as an effective and beneficial practice
- All participants rated efficacy of executive coaching at "moderately successful" or above
  - o 11 percent of programs were rated as "outstandingly successful"

- 67 percent (6 out of the 9 participants asked) estimated that benefits exceeded costs
- 5 out of 17 participants (29.4 percent) performed return-on-investment analyses following executive coaching interventions; of these 5, only 1 conducted a formal analysis
    o Most participants cited insufficient measurement tools as the reason for not conducting these analyses
- 88 percent indicated a "strong interest" in using executive coaches in the future
- Scheduling and cost were cited as the two biggest drawbacks to executive coaching
- Professional development was reported as the greatest gain from executive coaching

Originality / Value
- HR professionals provide valuable data, as they frequently encounter executive coaching practices, but still remain an external observer to the process
    o In contrast, most studies on executive coaching sample coaches or executives, who often have to justify or promote the coaching methods they have employed

Strengths
- Use of sound empirical techniques (i.e., structured interviews, large sample variance)
- Exploration of *why* executive coaching is effective

Limitations
- Small sample size ($N = 17$)
- Exploratory survey data prohibits causal conclusions
- Survey responses contain subjective and potentially biased opinions

Categories: T2, I, M, C11, P10

***

Dean, M. L., & Meyer, A. A. (2002). Executive coaching: In search of a model. *Journal of Leadership Education, 1,* **3–17.**

Relevant Sections: Overview, Coach and Client Characteristics

Purpose
- Provide an operational definition of executive coaching, examine the goals of coaching efforts, and outline important competencies for executive coaches

Design / Methodology
- Presents findings from coaching literature and applied practices
- Lays out common goals and competencies necessary for executive coaching

Findings / Implications
- Nearly all executive coaching practices are aimed at developing self-awareness, motivation, and interpersonal skills, while limiting counterproductive behaviors
- Executive coaches must possess skills and abilities such as developing rapport, assessment, providing feedback, overcoming resistance, motivating and engaging clients, stress management, a knowledge of business and organizational dynamics, integrity, and ethics
- These can be obtained through academic training, supervised experience, or business experience

Originality / Value
- Provides a list of important competencies for executive coaches, as well as how to develop those competencies

Strengths
- Emphasizes many of the similarities and differences that exist among definitions of executive coaching
- Addresses implications for executive coach training

Limitations
- Scant empirical research to support the list of executive coach competencies

Categories: T1, C20, P14

***

de Haan, E., Bertie, C., Day, A., & Sills, C. (in press). Critical moments of clients of coaching: Towards a 'client model' of executive coaching. In press at *Academy of Management Learning and Education*.

Relevant Sections: Coaching Process

Purpose
- Investigate whether coaching clients are aware of *critical moments* during coaching and, if so, how they experience these critical moments

Design / Methodology
- Administered a survey asking participants to describe a critical moment as a client

- 67 completed surveys (20 no-moments, 47 critical moments)
- Follow-up interviews with 8 participants (5 who responded they had experienced a critical moment and 3 who had not)
- Critical moments content coded

Findings / Implications
- New ways of understanding the client's experience of coaching as distinct from the coaches' experiences are warranted
- Two client distinctions in how they experienced coaching were identified:
    1. Incremental change versus transformational change
    2. Internal versus external processing
- Not all clients experience critical moments
- Critical moments involve new realizations (increased self-awareness)
- The coach was mentioned significantly more as contributing to the experience by respondents describing negative critical moments versus positive critical moments
- Clients and coaches report different phenomena in describing critical moments, with coaches focusing on emotions and anxieties versus clients' focus on outcomes and insight

Originality / Value
- Proposes a coaching model based on the client's perspective and experience of coaching
- Demonstrates the importance of the dynamics of the coach-client relationship
- Demonstrates the importance of reflexivity in coaching (ability to experience and reflect on one's inner world at times of heightened emotion)
- Explores the use of metaphors and the language clients use to describe critical moments

Strengths
- Examines coaching from the client's perspective
- Compares client data to coach data collected from a previous study
- Good detail regarding the process used to code data and develop a coaching model

Limitations
- Low response rate

Categories: T2, M, C46, P46

***

de Haan, E., Culpin, V., & Curd, J. (2011). Executive coaching in practice: What determines helpfulness for clients of coaching? *Personnel Review, 40*(1), 24–44.

Relevant Sections: Coaching Process

Purpose: Examine what aspects of coaches' behaviors and clients' learning styles determine the helpfulness of executive coaching for the client

Design / Methodology
- 71 participants completed a Web-based questionnaire shortly after beginning coaching, and 31 of those same participants six months later
- The questionnaire consisted of items from The Coaching Behaviors Questionnaire, The Learning Styles Inventory, and open-ended questions
- The independent variable was *helpfulness* (the degree to which coaching has positively impacted on the conscious mind of the client) and the dependent variables were coaching behaviors

Findings / Implications
- Clients experience helpfulness in a generic way: if they find the coaching helpful, they view a wide range of particular aspects of coaching as also helpful
- The three qualities most appreciated in a coach are listening, understanding, and encouragement
- Specific techniques don't impact perceptions of coach helpfulness but rather the coach's ability to use many techniques well and at the right time
- Coaches should consider shifting their focus from specific behaviors or techniques to an emphasis on the quality of the relationship with their client

Originality / Value
- Examines coaching through the subjective lens of the client
- Provides support for *common factors* in coaching (i.e., the general factors present in every coaching relationship such as expectation, motivation, quality of the relationship versus specific behaviors, models, or techniques)

Strengths
- Multiple quantitative measures were utilized
- Discusses the importance of supervising and training coaches based on the client's perspective of what's helpful rather than relying only on established techniques and coaching models

Limitations
- Small sample size
- Only the client's perspective is addressed
- No control group
- Methodology is only conducive for assessing the impact of executive coaching on individual outcomes and not organizational outcomes

Categories: T2, M, C29, P37

* * *

De Meuse, K. P., Dai, G., & Lee, R. J. (2009). Evaluating the effectiveness of executive coaching: Beyond ROI? *Coaching: An International Journal of Theory, Research and Practice, 2*(2), 117–134.

Relevant Sections: Coaching Outcomes

Purpose
- Conduct a meta-analysis of the effectiveness of executive coaching

Design / Methodology
- Reviewed the literature on evaluating executive coaching
- Meta-analyzed six studies
- Reviewed retrospective studies of coaching effectiveness

Findings / Implications
- Meta-analytic results suggested that coaching leads to an improvement in clients' performance ratings (as rated by clients and by others)
- Evaluations of coaching suggest executives and organizations have favorable opinions of coaching
- In addition to individual-level outcomes, coaching also impacts group-level outcomes such as team performance
- Evaluations of the return on investment from coaching vary across situations

Originality / Value
- Conducted a meta-analysis of the effectiveness of executive coaching

Strengths
- Good overview of current state of coaching evaluation studies

Limitations
- Limited number of primary studies suitable for inclusion in the meta-analysis

Categories: T3, I, C71, P17

* * *

Driscoll, M. (2005). E-mentoring and e-coaching. In M. Driscoll & S. Carliner (Eds.), *Advanced web-based training strategies: Unlocking instructionally sound online learning* **(pp. 187–206). San Francisco, CA: Pfeiffer & Company.**

Relevant Sections: Medium

Purpose
- Define and distinguish "e-coaching" and "e-mentoring"
- Outline benefits and drawbacks to e-learning strategies
- Suggest strategies for implementing e-mentoring or e-coaching programs
- Provide real-world example of an e-mentoring Web site

Design / Methodology
- Based on author's experiences and examples from other applied settings

Findings / Implications
- Coaching and mentoring differ along six dimensions: focus, role, relationship, source of influence, personal returns, and arena
- Benefits of virtual coaching and mentoring include accessibility, flexibility, cost efficiency, and a recorded log of communications
- Virtual mentoring and coaching are limited in that they are impersonal, can create a delay in communication, and require the appropriate technology and technological skills
- E-mentoring/e-coaching can be entirely virtual, blended, or simply a Web-based service to provide online learning
- E-mentoring/e-coaching programs should also consider the cultural match between coach and client

Originality / Value
- Tailored toward organizations or executives eager to implement an e-mentoring and/or e-coaching program
- Provides examples from actual e-coaching Web site (MentorNet)

Strengths
- Provides clear distinction between "mentor" and "coach"

Limitations
- The terms "mentor" and "coach" are still used interchangeably throughout the chapter
- Little empirical evidence

Categories: T5, I, C6, P20

***

Ducharme, M. J. (2004). The cognitive-behavioral approach to executive coaching. *Consulting Psychology Journal: Practice and Research,* *56*(4), 214–224.

Relevant Sections: Coaching Process

Purpose
- Examine the concepts, techniques, and theoretical underpinnings associated with cognitive behavioral therapy in terms of its applicability to executive coaching

Design / Methodology
- Identifies the unique aspects of interventions aimed at this high-performing client group
- Assesses whether the cognitive-behavioral approach (CBA) is appropriate and likely to be effective in the executive coaching context

Findings / Implications
- There are five unique aspects of executive coaching that must be taken into account:
  1. Success of coaching is measured in concrete and objective terms
  2. Individuals seek out coaching for new skills or to eliminate maladaptive behavior
  3. Executives have unique needs including dealing with high levels of stress
  4. Scope of executive coaching is broad and may require a variety of techniques
  5. Efficacy of cognitive behavioral therapy is well documented across a variety of populations
- Cognitive-behavioral coaching (CBC) is an intuitive approach likely to appeal to executives because of its simplicity and transparency
- CBC should be part of any coaching engagement dealing with the management of stress
- CBC is highly effective in situations when there is no reason to delve into an individual's psyche
- Limitations of CBC center around its simplicity, which may be seen by high-functioning clients as mechanical and unsophisticated
- These same reasons may draw some coach-client teams to the approach, i.e., its simplicity, ease of use, focus on results, efficacy, and goal orientation

Originality / Value
- The benefits of the CBA are discussed within the context of executive coaching

- Few authors have referred to a cognitive-behavioral perspective of coaching
- Provides a list of executive coaching goals that are met—e.g., measurable results, sustained change, stress management—and not met—e.g., wisdom development, self-awareness, systems approach—by CBC
- Calls attention to a different theoretical foundation for executive coaching

Strengths
- Discusses the practical value of CBC given the "specific and issue-focused" nature of this approach
- Strengths and weaknesses of CBC are discussed in a straightforward manner
- Discusses situations in which CBC is appropriate

Limitations: None noted

Categories: T1, C29, P11

✳ ✳ ✳

Ely, K., Boyce, L. A., Nelson, J. K., Zaccaro, S. J., Hernez-Broome, G., & Whyman, W. (2010). Evaluating leadership coaching: A review and integrated framework. *Leadership Quarterly, 21*(4), 585–599.

Relevant Sections: Coaching Outcomes

Purpose
- Review the academic and practitioner literature to understand how coaching engagements are being evaluated

Design / Methodology
- Reviewed 49 studies evaluating leadership coaching
- Coded studies based on methodologies, data sources, analysis approaches, and criteria used to evaluate coaching engagements

Findings / Implications
- Greater efforts are being made to conduct and report the findings of summative evaluations of leadership coaching (i.e., reactions, learning, behavior, and results)
- The most frequently assessed coaching outcome was self-reported changes in clients' leadership behaviors (82 percent of studies), followed by clients' perceptions of the effectiveness of coaching (49 percent of studies)

- The majority of studies are limited in their methodology and analyses—relying on post-coaching surveys and presenting descriptive statistics of findings

Originality / Value
- A two-pronged approach is proposed to evaluate coaching, focusing on both outcomes (summative evaluation) to assess coaching's effectiveness as a development intervention, and processes (formative evaluation) to account for the dynamic and customized nature of coaching
- Recommendations for future evaluation studies focus on examining changes in outcomes (e.g., pre- to post-performance), as well as the effects of different aspects of coaching (i.e., client, coach, client-coach relationship, and coaching processes) on coaching outcomes

Strengths
- Provides overview of how coaching engagements are being evaluated
- Provides comprehensive list of empirical coaching research studies with outcome-focused data

Limitations
- Only reviewed evaluation practices in published articles—may have missed segment of practitioners

Categories: T1, I, C113, P15

✳ ✳ ✳

Evers, W. J. G., Brouwers, A., & Tomic, W. (2006). A quasi-experimental study on management coaching effectiveness. *Consulting Psychology Journal: Practice and Research, 58,* **174–182.**

Relevant Sections: Coaching Outcomes

Purpose
- Examine whether coaching increases managers' self-efficacy and outcome expectancies

Design / Methodology
- Quasi-experimental study used a pre/post design with a control group
- Sample included 60 managers—30 managers about to undergo coaching were matched to a control group of 30 participants not undergoing coaching
- A survey was administered at two points in time—initially (prior to the experimental group's coaching engagements) and again four months later

- Six measures included in survey assessed clients':
  1. Self-efficacy for goal setting
  2. Self-efficacy for acting in balanced way
  3. Self-efficacy for mindful living and working
  4. Outcome expectancies for goal setting
  5. Outcome expectancies for acting in a balanced way
  6. Outcome expectancies for mindful living and working

Findings / Implications

- Experimental group showed significant increases in two of the six variables measured: (1) self-efficacy for goal setting ($F = 4.18$) and (2) outcome expectancies for acting in a balanced way ($F = 5.05$)

Originality / Value

- Provides initial evidence of the effectiveness of coaching via increased self-efficacy and outcome expectancies

Strengths

- Pre/post design with control group

Limitations

- Relies on self-report data from clients

Categories: T2, C19, P9

* * *

Feldman, D. C., & Lankau, M. J. (2005). Executive coaching: A review and agenda for future research. *Journal of Management, 31,* 829–848.

Relevant Sections: Overview

Purpose

- Review the current executive coaching literature, as well as executive practices and their impact on organizations
- Article encourages more rigorous research in order to identify and confirm the factors, processes, and outcomes relevant to executive coaching

Design / Methodology

- Examines the empirical research and coaching best practices of the recent decade (1995–2005)

Findings / Implications

- Executive coaching defined as a dyadic relationship that provides the executive (often a mid- to senior-level manager) with constructive feedback and strategies to improve performance

- Coaching is a distinct construct from therapy, advising, mentoring, or career counseling
- Executive coaching entails data gathering, feedback, periodic coaching sessions, and evaluation
  - While these phases are generally the same across practices, many different approaches can be taken, as executive coaches stem from a wide array of backgrounds

Originality / Value
- Integrates both empirical and applied findings on executive coaching in order to outline agenda for future research

Strengths
- Encourages future research to identify what aspects of each process produce positive and negative outcomes

Limitations
- Cursory explanation of different approaches to the coaching process and the advantages and disadvantages associated with each

Categories: T3, I, C75, P19

✳ ✳ ✳

Garman, A. N., Whiston, D. L., & Zlatoper, K. W. (2000). Media perceptions of executive coaching and the formal preparation of coaches. *Consulting Psychology Journal: Practice and Research, 52,* **201–205.**

Relevant Sections: Coach and Client Characteristics

Purpose
- Public perceptions of executive coaching examined through assessing how executive coaching was portrayed in mainstream and trade management publications

Design / Methodology
- Executive coaching articles appearing in mainstream and trade management publications between 1991 and 1998 were content coded
- Initial pool of 72 articles was identified and content coded
  - 40 articles discussed external coaching
  - 32 articles discussed internal coaching

Findings / Implications
- Media stories on executive coaching increased in number in the time frame considered

- Vast majority of articles (88 percent) presented coaching very favorably
- Only 31 percent of articles provided any mention of coaches as having psychological training
    - Psychology was mentioned less frequently over the time period considered
- Psychology was primarily mentioned in relation to providing a unique skill base for coaching 61 percent of the time it appeared in articles
    - Psychological skill base was viewed as being favorable 45 percent of the time
        - Potentially favorable or unfavorable 36 percent
        - Potentially harmful 18 percent
- When articles discussed selecting a coach, they rarely mentioned selecting someone familiar with assessment tools
- Articles discussing the selection of a coach focused mostly on past experience and "fit"

Originality / Value
- Examines executive coaching from the perspective of nonpractitioners
- Examines extent to which psychologists have been identified as providers of coaching services
- Examines perceptions of psychologists as executive coaches

Strengths
- Provides an overview of how executive coaching has been discussed in the media

Limitations
- More detail in how articles were coded would be helpful
- Additional research needed to evaluate perceptions of coaching and the preferred preparation of coaches through more direct means such as interviewing or surveying people considering selecting a coach

Categories: T2, C10, P5

***

Goldsmith, M. (2006). E-coaching: Using the new technology to develop tomorrow's leaders. In M. Goldsmith & L. S. Lyons (Eds.), *Coaching for leadership: The practice of leadership coaching from the world's greatest coaches* (2nd ed., pp. 213–220). San Francisco, CA: Pfeiffer & Company.

Relevant Sections: Medium

Purpose
- Outline advantages and disadvantages of the increasingly global and technological business world as they relate to coaching practices
- Identify steps required to implement effective e-coaching practices

Design / Methodology
- Based on the author's personal experiences and research

Findings / Implications
- The increasingly global network of the future creates the following advantages for coaching practices:
    - A wider range of leaders and experts will be readily accessible
    - Development tools can be tailored to meet specific individual needs
    - International communication is possible without the restrictions of time zones or traveling costs
    - "Push" technology can provide frequent monitoring and motivation for coachees
- The global network poses the following challenges for the e-coaching process:
    - Coaches and coachees can become overloaded with the amount of (often irrelevant) information available
    - Difficult to develop technological tools that can easily deliver effective coaching
    - Immediacy and breadth of information could discourage deeper thought processes
    - Access to the same information could create homogeneous leaders
- The following processes will be required of the "e-coach of the future"
    - Diagnosing a client's needs in terms of development, depth, and urgency
    - Assessing a client's resources (e.g., time, money, technology)
    - Understanding the costs and benefits of a wide array of learning options
    - Connecting leaders with useful resources and opportunities
    - Providing continuous guidance and information to leaders

Originality / Value
- Identifies specific tasks, challenges, knowledge, and responsibilities required of the e-coach of the future
- Implies that e-coaches of the future will be responsible for finding valuable information and resources, rather than directly providing them

Strengths
- Provides specific, practice-based applications
- Identifies unique challenges to e-coaching practices

Limitations
- No definition of e-coaching
- Little empirical basis

Categories: T5, C0, P8

***

Grant, A. M., Curtayne, L., & Burton, G. (2009). Executive coaching enhances goal attainment, resilience and workplace well-being: A randomised controlled study. *The Journal of Positive Psychology, 4*(5), 396–407.

Relevant Sections: Coaching Outcomes

Purpose
- Examine the impact of executive coaching on executives' goal attainment, resilience, and well-being in a randomized controlled study

Design / Methodology
- Randomized controlled study in a large health agency in Australia
    - Participants included 41 (of 50) executives and senior managers who participated in a leadership development program
    - 38 females and 3 males; mean age of 49.84 years
    - Randomized controlled-waitlist design; measures beginning of development program, 10 weeks, and 20 weeks later; group 1 completed coaching and measures at 10 weeks; group 2 completed coaching and measures at 20 weeks
    - Leadership development program consisted of multisource feedback, one half-day leadership training workshop, and four individual coaching sessions
    - Quantitative and open-ended measures used (goal attainment, resilience, depression, and workplace well-being)

Findings / Implications
- Goal attainment scores increased at the end of individual coaching sessions
- Resilience scores increased at the conclusion of individual coaching sessions
- Some evidence that depression, stress, and anxiety scores decreased at the conclusion of individual coaching sessions
- Workplace well-being scores increased at the conclusion of individual coaching sessions
- Qualitative comments were coded and reflected increased confidence, increased ability to deal with organizational change, personal or professional insights, and assistance in finding ways to develop client's career

Originality / Value
- Randomized controlled study

Strengths
- Examines a variety of outcomes hypothesized to be influenced by coaching
- Evidence that as little as four coaching sessions can influence important outcomes

Limitations
- Executives in this population had received very little leadership development previously; coaching may have been effective in part because participants had not received intensive leadership development previously
- Need to identify the mechanisms by which well-being and other outcomes are influenced by coaching
- All data provided from a single source (self-report)

Categories: T2, C52, P12

*** * ****

Gyllensten, K., & Palmer, S. (2007). The coaching relationship: An interpretative phenomenological analysis. *International Coaching Psychology Review, 2*(2), 168–177.

Relevant Sections: Coaching Process, Coach-Client Matching

Purpose
- Investigate client experiences and views of the coaching process

Design / Methodology
- Qualitative study using Interpretive Phenomenological Analysis (IPA)
- Nine clients from two large organizations interviewed about their experiences
    - Three males, six females (mean age of 33 years); four held management positions
    - United Kingdom finance and Scandinavian telecom organizations (3,000-plus employees)

Findings / Implications
- Identified coaching relationship as a major but not the only factor of useful coaching
- Coaching relationship was valuable to clients and this relationship was dependent on trust and improved by transparency
    - Confidentiality helped build a relationship of trust
    - Transparency led clients to feel included in the coaching process, which might have a positive effect on subsequent commitment to the coaching
- Working toward goals and improving performance also identified as important factors
- Impresses the importance of coaches being aware of and working with the coaching relationship, particularly at the start of the coaching

Originality / Value
- Indicates that unless "a good enough relationship was developed in the coaching, relevant achievements would not be made" (p. 175)
    - Positive atmosphere needs to be developed from the beginning of coaching for client to feel comfortable and share information
    - Improves likelihood that the client will continue with the coaching and consequently gain something from it
- Results discussed in terms of previous literature

Strengths
- Provides a step-by-step description of IPA; Interview Outline at Appendix
- Shares the researchers' interpretative framework and influences
- Presents a rich description of coaching relationships, including interview quotes

Limitations
- Article does not present a priori hypotheses, though authors acknowledge that the influence of their personal frame of reference influences their subjective analysis
- No details provided on the criteria used to select participants

- Article focuses on a portion of a larger piece of research on coaching and stress, which was mentioned but not explained

Categories: T2 I, C20, P10

✶ ✶ ✶

Hakim, C. (2003). Virtual coaching: Learning, like time, stops for no one. *The Journal for Quality and Participation, 23,* 42–44.

Relevant Sections: Medium

Purpose
- Outline the benefits of virtual coaching and explain how organizations can begin to implement e-coaching efforts

Design / Methodology
- Presents a list of benefits and processes of electronic executive coaching, based on the author's experiences as an executive coach

Findings / Implications
- Virtual coaching can be met with apprehension or resistance, as clients may not fully trust the effectiveness or confidentiality of the system
  - Coaches will need to work hard to address these concerns
- Benefits of virtual coaching include saving time, supporting ambiguity, building confidence, sharpening communication, allowing for quick "check-ins," and converting abstract ideas into concrete goals
- Over time, coachees can learn from their experiences and coach others

Originality / Value
- Provides specific direction for setting up blended coaching strategies

Strengths
- Provides a good definition of virtual coaching

Limitations
- As a coach, author is biased toward practice of coaching and does not address potential drawbacks

Categories: T5, C0, P3

✶ ✶ ✶

Hall, D. T., Otazo, K. L., & Hollenbeck, G. P. (1999). Behind closed doors: What really happens in executive coaching. *Organizational Dynamics, 27*(3), 39–53.

Relevant Sections: Coach and Client Characteristics, Organizational Support

Purpose
- Review aspects of the executive coaching process

Design / Methodology
- Interviews conducted with more than 75 executives in Fortune 100 companies and 15 executive coaches
- Participants were randomly selected from a list of individuals involved in executive coaching from organizations participating in the study

Findings / Implications
- Trust in coach is critical
- Internal coaches
  - Pros: Accessibility; opportunity to develop trust over time; in-depth knowledge of organization
  - Cons: May have conflicting interest between coachee and the organization
- External coaches
  - Pros: Provide strict confidentiality; objectivity; can say the "unspeakable"
- Important characteristics of a coach from coachee's perspective
  - Provides honest and challenging feedback
  - Good listening skills
  - Provides good action ideas
  - Accessible
  - Not guided by personal agenda
  - Competence
- Important characteristics of a coach from coach's perspective
  - Strong connection and personal relationship with client
  - Good listening skills
  - Caring
  - Holds client accountable
  - Demonstrates honesty and integrity
- Concerns related to the future of executive coaching
  - Managing demand for executive coaching
  - Addressing ethical issues related to conflict of interest (for internal coaches)
  - Controlling costs of executive coaching

Originality / Value
- Provides a good overview of the state of the practice of executive coaching

Strengths
- Provides perspective of both coaches and clients
- Provides a good overview of issues in the practice of executive coaching

Limitations
- Limited information on the study sample and how information was gained from interviews

Categories: T2, C0, P14

✳ ✳ ✳

Hamilton, B. A., & Scandura, T. A. (2003). E-mentoring: Implications for organizational learning and development in a wired world. *Organizational Dynamics, 31,* **388–402.**

Relevant Sections: Medium

Purpose
- Examine the benefits and challenges of electronic mentoring (e-mentoring)
- Discuss ways to incorporate technology into mentoring practices

Design / Methodology
- Presents dimensions and benefits of e-mentoring

Findings / Implications
- E-mentoring provides greater scheduling flexibility and increased accessibility to mentors
  - Can overcome organizational, individual, interpersonal, and scheduling barriers
- Especially useful as a supplement to traditional mentoring practices
- Progresses through the same phases of "initiation, cultivation, and separation" as traditional mentoring processes
- Technological factors (i.e., situational factors, social factors, usefulness, ease of use) moderate the effectiveness of e-mentoring
  - Technology can also interact with individual factors such as gender, ethnicity, age, and personality
  - E-mentors and mentees will need virtual communication skills, as they cannot rely on body language or visual cues for communication

- Implementation of an e-mentoring program requires a technology infrastructure, training, managerial support, establishing goals and expectations, and selection procedures

Originality / Value
- Highlights the values of e-mentoring in terms of reducing the effects of social biases

Strengths
- Provides clear definition of e-mentoring

Limitations
- Does not discuss the drawbacks of e-mentoring
- Findings and implications are not based on empirical evidence

Categories: T5, I, C0, P15

✳ ✳ ✳

Hernez-Broome, G., & Hughes, L. (2004). Leadership development: Past, present and future. *Human Resource Planning, 27,* **24–32.**

Relevant Sections: Overview, Organizational Support

Purpose
- Examine leadership development trends over the past 20 years, current trends in executive coaching practices, and predicted trends that globalization and technology will bring

Design / Methodology
- Outlines common leadership development practices of the past 20 years
- Describes several themes in present-day executive coaching practices
- Based on past and present trends, outlines future challenges in the practice of executive coaching

Findings / Implications
- In the past two decades, leadership development has become increasingly focused on team research, leader interpersonal skills, and active learning techniques
- Current literature and practices focus on leader-follower interactions, competency development, work-life balance, and leadership development in the context of the workplace
- Globalization and technology of the future will create increased emphasis on:
    - Leader integrity and ethics
    - Deep understanding of executive coaching processes

    o Quantitative methods for calculating executive coaching benefits

Originality / Value
- Integrates past and current practices to pinpoint how executive coaching has developed and how it will need to adapt for the future

Strengths
- Provides concise history of executive coaching
- Outlines practices and challenges that may be relevant to the future

Limitations
- Little emphasis on the past, present, and future of empirical research in executive coaching

Categories: T1, C45, P8

✳ ✳ ✳

Hollenbeck, G. P. (2002). Coaching executives: Individual leader development. In R. Silzer (Ed.), *The 21st century executive: Innovative practices for building leadership at the top* (pp. 137–167). San Francisco, CA: Jossey-Bass.

Relevant Sections: Coach-Client Matching, Coach and Client Characteristics, Overview

Purpose
- Identify and discuss issues and trends in coaching; addresses following topics:
  - o How companies use executive coaching
  - o Where coaching comes from and why it is so popular
  - o What executive coaches do and how executive coaching differs from lifestyle or personal coaching and psychotherapy
  - o Does executive coaching work?
  - o What can organizations and executives do to make the best use of coaching?
- Target HR audience; focus is *about* coaching executives, not *how* to coach them

Design / Methodology
- Responds to the questions based on relevant research, personal experience, interviews with subject-matter-experts, and review of various organizational practices

Findings / Implications
- Large organizations with a coaching pool are concerned with fit of the coach with the organization and coaching competence
  - o Coach screening includes review of résumé, screening survey (Figure 3), interviews, reference checks
  - o Example of interview topics include coach's definition and approach to coaching, previous assignments accepted or rejected, orientation, and flexibility
- Emphasizes the importance of a good match
  - o Defines "right" in terms of expertise and style
  - o Can be achieved by allowing clients to choose from several coach options, referred to as "the beauty contest" (p. 160)

Originality / Value
- Provides an experience-based discussion regarding how organizations select coaches and match them with executives, using examples

Strengths
- Stipulates that they know of no research that prescribes a scientific process for ensuring a good coach-client fit

Limitations
- Addresses a number of coaching issues briefly rather than examining a few in greater detail

Categories: T5, I, C24, P30

✳ ✳ ✳

Homan, M., & Miller, L. J. (2008). Developing master coaching skills. In *Coaching in organizations: Best coaching practices from the Ken Blanchard Companies* (pp. 181–209). San Francisco, CA: John Wiley and Sons.

Relevant Sections: Coach-Client Matching, Coach and Client Characteristics, Organizational Support

Purpose
- Define and describe coaching competencies

Design / Methodology
- Presents insights based on authors' "years of experience in recruiting and deploying coaches" (p. 182)

Findings / Implications
- Four categories of coaching competencies: General, Corporate, Executive, Master
  - General: basic competencies, such as ability to build trust, listen, offer feedback
  - Corporate: competencies needed for coaches working in an organization
  - Executive: competencies needed for coaching top-level members of organizations
  - Master: competencies needed for coaches coaching coaches
- Ability to match personal style with client style (General competency)
  - Coaches should be able to match the client's style preference
  - Coaches should, if needed, influence client's style preference
  - Style issues include: energy, thinking style and speed, and humor

Originality / Value
- Provides perspective of experienced practitioners regarding match factors

Strengths
- Discussion presented succinctly

Limitations
- Minimal inclusion of examples to illustrate concepts or outside evidence to support competency inclusion

Categories: T5, C1, P28

✳ ✳ ✳

Hooijberg, R., & Lane, N. (2009). Using multisource feedback coaching effectively in executive education. *Academy of Management Learning & Education, 8*(4), 483–493.

Relevant Sections: Coach and Client Characteristics, Coaching Process, Coaching Outcomes

Purpose
- Examine what coaches do in executive education programs to foster behavior change

Design / Methodology
- Open-ended survey administered to managers in eight different executive education programs at a leading European business school

      o Questions asked about effective coaching, obstacles and facilitators of implementing action plans, and behavior changes made as a result of coaching

      o Survey mailed to 700 managers; 232 managers participated (33 percent response rate)

      o 82 percent male; 84 percent between 35 and 54 years old

      o Grounded theory approach used to identify major categories and subcategories

Findings / Implications

- Perceptions of what determines effective coaching
  - Client responsibility, coaches' skills, and chemistry (33 percent of responses)
  - Coach professionalism, interpretation of results, and inspiring action (85 percent)
  - Most important coaches' skills identified: giving recommendations, interpreting results, and helping assimilate feedback
- Perceptions of whether coaching leads to change
  - Almost all participants (97.4 percent) reported leaving multi-source feedback session having identified 1 to 3 issues or areas to work on and somewhat high or high commitment (81 percent) to work on the issues identified
  - A majority (61 percent) reported working on their identified issues in their workplace
- Perceived obstacles to coaching effectiveness
  - Clients themselves, including attitude and habits (27.3 percent)
  - Lack of time (21.1 percent) and daily routine (15.7 percent)
- Perceived facilitators of implementing action or development plans
  - Clients themselves, including changing one's mind-set and seeing positive results (37.1 percent), other people (19.2 percent), and actions taken (14.1 percent)

Originality / Value

- Examines what coaches actually do to facilitate behavior change
- Highlights importance of context in which coaching occurs

Strengths

- Explores what coaches actually do that facilitates performance improvement in clients
- Highlights need to consider the context in which coaching occurs

Limitations

- Research is primarily exploratory in nature

- Multisource feedback and coaching occurred as part of a broader executive education program, creating an alternative explanation for the results observed
- All data provided from a single source and at a single point in time (self-report)

Categories: T2, I, C23, P11

✻ ✻ ✻

Jay, M. (2003). Understanding how to leverage executive coaching.
Organization Development Journal, 21, **6–19.**

Relevant Sections: Overview, Coaching Outcomes, Coaching Process

Purpose
- Assess how to leverage executive coaching practices by incorporating emotional intelligence and "fourth-loop learning" into the coaching process
- Define aspects of emotional intelligence and how these aspects can be applied to executive coaching

Design / Methodology
- A conceptual model is derived from common coaching practices and the author's own expertise and experiences
- Extends previous research on emotional intelligence by Goleman (1988)

Findings / Implications
- Coaching practices should increase emotional intelligence in order to provide coachees with the advanced social skills to understand and subsequently manage behaviors
- Article outlines the definitions and uses of single-, double-, triple-, and fourth-loop learning
  - Single-loop learning involves aligning behaviors with expectations
  - Double-loop learning considers the variables that may be causing discrepancies between behaviors and expectations
  - Triple-loop learning requires the learner to view his or her own actions objectively
    - This can fully address the internal, external, financial, and developmental domains of the business system

  o Through fourth-loop learning, coachees simultaneously process the behaviors, expectations, identities, and governing variables that exist among parallel systems or streams of consciousness
    – Achieves the most leverage in executive coaching practices

Originality / Value

- Extends Goleman's (1988) emotional intelligence typology in order to identify ways to leverage executive coaching

Strengths

- Defines emotional intelligence

Limitations

- Strategy-focused approach could be supplemented with recommendations for implementation

Categories: T5, I, C11, P13

✳ ✳ ✳

Jones, R. A., Rafferty, A. E., & Griffin, M. A. (2006). The executive coaching trend: Towards more flexible executives. *Leadership & Organization Development Journal, 27,* **584–596.**

Relevant Sections: Coaching Outcomes

Purpose

- Investigate the influence of leadership coaching on executives' managerial flexibility

Design / Methodology

- Empirical study surveyed 46 executives who participated in a leadership development program that included 360-degree feedback, leadership workshops, and coaching
- All clients participating in the coaching received six one-hour coaching sessions every two weeks for three months
- A 10-item measure of flexibility was administered to clients prior to coaching, halfway through the coaching engagement (after session three), and post coaching (after session six)
- 11 executives provided survey data at all three points in time

Findings / Implications

- Clients' flexibility increased over time ($F = 2.56$)

Originality / Value
- Provides initial support for the positive effect of coaching on flexibility

Strengths
- Longitudinal design

Limitations
- Small sample size
- Relies on self-report data

Categories: T2, C33, P13

✶ ✶ ✶

Joo, B. (2005). Executive coaching: A conceptual framework from an integrative review of practice and research. *Human Resource Development Review, 4,* **462–488.**

Relevant Sections: Overview

Purpose
- Integrate empirical research and literature from other practices to identify gaps in executive coaching literature
- Develop conceptual framework as a context in which to address the gaps

Design / Methodology
- Reviews 78 articles from both academic and practice journals, business magazines, and book chapters
- Articles were categorized according to their source, methodology, definition, and focus
  - Majority of articles came from practice-focused journals (74 percent) and the organizational/business management literature (60 percent).
  - 11 research articles were found, only 6 of which employed quantitative methods

Findings / Implications
- Outlines an I-P-O framework for executive coaching
  - Inputs include characteristics of the coach, coachee, and organization
  - Processes include the coaching approach, coachee receptivity, and the overall quality of the coach-coachee relationship
  - Outcomes can be proximal, such as self-awareness and learning, or distal, such as individual and organizational success

Originality / Value
- Integrates executive coaching practices and literature to develop a conceptual framework

Strengths
- Provides a starting point for rigorous and relevant executive coaching research

Limitations
- Does not address possible moderators within the proposed framework
- Framework should be expanded to assess effects of time, contexts, and measurements

Categories: T1, M, C60, P26

✳ ✳ ✳

Kampa-Kokesch, S., & Anderson, M. Z. (2001). Executive coaching: A comprehensive review of the literature. *Consulting Psychology Journal: Practice and Research, 53,* **205–228.**

Relevant Sections: Overview, Coaching Outcomes

Purpose
- Identify which aspects of executive coaching are confirmed by research and which require further empirical backing

Design / Methodology
- Reviews literature on the history of executive coaching and current practices
- Outlines various definitions, techniques, and purposes of executive coaching, the characteristics of coaches and clients, and the distinction between coaching and counseling
- Describes the purpose, method, findings, and implications of seven empirical studies of executive coaching

Findings / Implications
- Identifies six themes in the practice literature that are confirmed by empirical findings
    1. Executive coaching benefits both the client and the client's organization
    2. Executive coaching increases the client's learning
    3. Behavioral changes in the client can occur through executive coaching
    4. Executive coaches have a variety of backgrounds

    5. Executive coaching involves a variety of methods

    6. Executive coaching can be used for both remedial and developmental purposes

Originality / Value
- Highlights areas where empirical research and actual practices overlap and where they are incomplete

Strengths
- Provides concise summary of what is known in the field of executive coaching
- Encourages future research in order to create a consensus on definition and best practices of executive coaching

Limitations
- Most references collected from applied (rather than empirical) journals

Categories: T3, I, M, C90, P23

✳ ✳ ✳

Kaspirin, C. A., Single, P. B., Single, R. M., & Muller, C. B. (2003). Building a better bridge: Testing e-training to improve e-mentoring programmes in higher education. *Mentoring & Tutoring, 11*(1), 67–78.

Relevant Sections: Medium

Purpose
- Develop and test the effects of an e-training program on satisfaction, involvement, and perceived value

Design / Methodology
- 400 undergraduate students randomly assigned to an experimental or control condition
  - Experimental condition participants were required to complete online training; control condition participants were told that online training was optional
- Subjects were given surveys and matched with a mentor
- Mentors and subjects interacted electronically using the MentorNet program
- Measures were collected from participants at the end of the academic year

Findings / Implications
- Findings show the benefits of e-training before entering into an e-mentoring relationship

- Subjects in the experimental group demonstrated significantly more involvement
    - o Involvement was operationalized by the frequency of e-mails
- No significant differences between groups regarding satisfaction or perceived value
- Identifies moderating effect of mandatory participation on e-mentoring outcomes

Originality / Value
- One of the earliest studies to assess e-mentoring efficacy and user perceptions

Strengths
- Highlights the importance of online training programs for electronic coaches and clients
- Focuses on client reactions to required training and how these reactions might influence future coaching participation

Limitations
- Increased involvement of experimental group could have been due to mandatory nature of assignment rather than increased satisfaction or efficacy
- Non-significant findings for satisfaction and perceived value could have been due to ceiling effect, as all participants rated e-mentoring programs as very high on both dimensions

Categories: T2, I, M, C21, P12

* * *

Kilburg, R. R. (2004). When shadows fall: Using psychodynamic approaches in executive coaching. *Consulting Psychology Journal: Practice and Research, 56*(4), 246–268.

Relevant Sections: Coaching Process

Purpose
- Explore how events, feelings, thoughts, and patterns of behavior outside the individual's conscious awareness can significantly influence what executives decide and how they behave
- Review situations in which psychodynamic issues and interventions are relevant for executive coaches to consider

Design / Methodology
- Outlines 15 situations in which psychodynamic issues and interventions are relevant for executive coaching, such as when the client seeks to understand his or her history, goals, motives, and behaviors with a greater degree of psychological sophistication or when knowledge, skill, and ability may be insufficient to master a challenge

Findings / Implications
- Executive coaches would be "foolhardy" to use an approach that does not take into account the existence of unconscious mental, emotional, and social processes and how they affect the executives they coach
- Conflict and object relation approaches to understanding psychodynamics have a high degree of relevance for executive coaching
- Many psychotherapy methods are transferable to executive coaching
- Many coaches do not possess the competencies to use this approach competently, and many coaching situations do not call for such approaches
- A situation can be made worse by using this approach, especially in time-limited coaching engagements, since strong feelings may be surfaced and can produce wounds difficult to manage in the context of fast-paced organizations
- Identifies self-awareness, emotional management, and behavioral flexibility as types of development best suited to a psychodynamic approach to executive coaching

Originality / Value
- Describes the purposes of psychodynamic approaches and interventions in executive coaching
- Provides a concise summary of how unconscious psychological conflict affects executive performance

Strengths
- Describes a variety of intervention approaches coaches can use to approach psychodynamic material with clients
- Reviews limitations using these concepts and methods in executive coaching
- Provides numerous tables that summarize key issues important to consider when applying a psychodynamic approach to executive coaching
    - Appropriate executive coaching situations
    - Coaching methods
    - Stages of a behavioral or psychodynamic interpretation in executive coaching

         o Principles underlying interpretation
         o Pitfalls and limitations

Limitations: None noted

Categories: T1, C43, P23

∗ ∗ ∗

Knouse, S. B. (2001). Virtual mentors: Mentoring on the Internet. *Journal of Employment Counseling, 38,* 162–169.

Relevant Sections: Medium

Purpose
- Discuss the advantages of virtual mentoring
- Provide examples of successful virtual mentoring

Design / Methodology
- Reviews empirical and practice literature, as well as current Internet mentoring programs

Findings / Implications
- Online mentoring holds benefits over traditional face-to-face mentoring, such as accessibility, anonymity, and cost effectiveness
- There has been an increase in mentoring Web sites tailored to women, minorities, students, and the military.
  - o Also an increase in Web sites specifically for coaching purposes
- Online mentors are less able to monitor their clients and track their progress
- Future mentoring applications should include team virtual mentoring, group mentoring, and networking

Originality / Value
- Identifies research and examples of proven-effective virtual mentoring efforts

Strengths
- Provides evidence for the rise in virtual mentoring practices
- Draws on both academic and applied literature

Limitations
- Does not fully address differences between mentoring and coaching, or how virtual coaching might extend coaching practices

Categories: T3, C27, P7

∗ ∗ ∗

Kochanowski, S., Seifert, C. F., & Yukl, G. (2010). Using coaching to enhance the effects of behavioral feedback to managers. *Journal of Leadership & Organizational Studies, 17*(4), 363–369.

Relevant Sections: Coaching Outcomes, Organizational Support

Purpose
- Assess whether coaching enhances the effectiveness of a feedback workshop on managers' use of four influence tactics

Design / Methodology
- Field study with managers of a midsize grocery store chain
  - 30 store managers randomly assigned to one of two conditions
  - 56 subordinates in coaching condition
  - 37 subordinates in control condition
- Pre/post measure: Influence Behavior Questionnaire (IBQ)
  - Post-survey administered three months after coaching intervention
  - Feedback workshop training evaluation assessed workshop effectiveness
- Feedback workshop: six hours of IBQ feedback, inform and practice influence tactics
- Coaching: five 30-minute weekly telephone conversations and final one-hour face-to-face

Findings / Implications
- Follow-up coaching enhanced the effects of feedback on the use of collaboration with subordinates more than managers who did not receive coaching ($F = 4.31, p < .05$)
- No significant effects ($p < .05$) were found for rational persuasion, inspirational appeal, and consultation

Originality / Value
- Provides preliminary evidence of coaching impact over multisource feedback

Strengths
- Examined workshop ratings between experimental and control groups (no differences)
- Discussion highlights the role of organizational support and climate

Limitations
- Final sample size is not specified, although a high attrition rate is acknowledged
- Only feedback from subordinates examined

- Pre-measure differences between experimental and control groups not discussed
- Comparisons of managers included versus not included in final analysis not discussed

Categories: T2, M, C30, P7

* * *

Kombarakaran, F. A., Yang, J. A., Baker, M. N., & Fernandes, P. B. (2008). Executive coaching: It works! *Consulting Psychology Journal: Practice and Research, 60,* **78–90.**

Relevant Sections: Coaching Outcomes

Purpose
- Examine the effectiveness of a coaching initiative in a global pharmaceutical company

Design / Methodology
- Surveyed 42 coaches who had coached 114 executives in a large multinational organization over a six-month period
- After coaching, clients responded to 65 items on their perceptions of their coaching engagement, including both quantitative (on a 5-point Likert scale) and qualitative (short-answer) questions developed by the authors
- Coaches also completed surveys on their perceptions of the coaching engagements

Findings / Implications
- Based on the qualitative comments, five areas of change resulting from coaching were identified:
    1. People management
    2. Relationships with managers
    3. Goal setting and prioritization
    4. Engagement and productivity
    5. Effective communication
- 72 percent of the clients reported that coaching increased their confidence and 78 percent reported that coaching maximized their contribution to the company
- A review of the coaches' qualitative comments suggested that coaching increased clients' communication skills and effectiveness in their leadership roles

Originality / Value
- Documents the positive short-term effects of coaching

Strengths
- Collected multisource data (from clients and coaches)

Limitations
- No control group

Categories: T2, C19, P13

* * *

Latham, G. P. (2007). Theory and research on coaching practices.
Australian Psychologist, 42(4), 268–270.

Relevant Sections: Overview, Coach and Client Characteristics, Coaching
Process

Purpose
- Explicitly link coaching practices to existing psychological frameworks and empirical research to help develop an evidence-based approach to coaching

Design / Methodology
- Conceptual paper articulating the need to advance coaching practices
  and research
- Includes research examples to support suggested theories to apply

Findings / Implications
- Provides three theories that can be adapted to inform coaching research
    1. Dweck's Implicit Personal Theory (Heslin, VandeWalle, &
       Latham, 2006)
    2. Locke and Latham's Goal Theory (Locke & Latham, 2002;
       Heslin & Latham, 2004)
    3. Sociocognitive Theories (Sue-Chan & Latham, 2004; Brown &
       Latham, 2006)

Originality / Value
- Proposes that the application of findings from empirical research
  guided by theories will be more useful to the practicing community

Strengths
- Provides examples to support evidence-based management on
  coaching

Limitations
- Examples of theory-based research are not all leadership-coaching specific

Categories: T5, C20, P3

$$* * *$$

Levenson, A. (2009). Measuring and maximizing the business impact of executive coaching. *Consulting Psychology Journal: Practice and Research, 61,* **103–121.**

Relevant Sections: Coaching Outcomes

Purpose
- Examine coaching outcomes and outline conceptual and methodological issues related to assessing the impact of coaching
- Present a conceptual framework for identifying the factors related to organizational effectiveness
- Propose that coaching engagements directly impact leadership behaviors, which in turn influence business performance via outcomes that matter to the organization

Design / Methodology
- Examines 12 coaching engagements that had been rated as successful based on improvements in leadership behaviors
- Sample included 12 clients included in the study working at large firms in the consumer products, financial services, or health care industries
- Author interviewed the 10 coaches and 12 clients involved in the coaching engagements

Findings / Implications
- Participants found it challenging to identify direct impacts of their coaching engagements on business outcomes
- In order to assess the impact of coaching on business outcomes, it is important to account for the complexity of the leader's operating environment as well as the operating environment of the leader's team

Originality / Value
- Presents conceptual framework for evaluating the outcomes of coaching engagements

Strengths
- Multisource data (coaches and clients)

Limitations
- Small sample size

Categories: T4, I, C59, P19

❋ ❋ ❋

Liljenstrand, A. M., & Nebeker, D. M. (2008). Coaching services: A look at coaches, clients, and practices. *Consulting Psychology Journal: Practice and Research, 60*(1), 57–77.

Relevant Sections: Coach and Client Characteristics, Coaching Process

Purpose
- Explore how academic background of coach influences executive coaching

Design / Methodology
- Nine thousand coaches accessed through a variety of coaching organizations and associations were contacted and asked to participate in online survey
- Final $N = 2{,}231$ coaches

Findings / Implications
- Coaches' Personal Attributes
    - Coaches with a background in education, clinical psychology, or industrial/organizational psychology tended to be older
    - Majority of coaches were female (67 percent)
    - More coaching experience and education reported by psychologists
    - Prior career experience was rated as the most important preparation
    - Academic background reported as most useful preparation by psychologists; coaching training programs reported as most useful by other fields
    - Certification/licensure perceived as more important by business, other, and education backgrounds than by psychologists
    - All backgrounds strongly endorsed the need to adhere to ethical guidelines
- Client Attributes
    - Academic background influenced to which industry services provided
    - Business, education, and other backgrounds were most likely to coach entrepreneurs

- o Industrial/organizational psychologists were most likely to coach midlevel and top managers
- Delivery Practices
  - o Background of the coach influenced the goals they were hired to help clients achieve
    - – Business background: interpersonal relations
    - – Psychology background: communication and listening skills
    - – Education and other background: balancing work and professional life
  - o Assessment tools differed according to coach background
  - o Coaching formats differed by academic background

Originality / Value
- Examines influence of the coach's background in executive coaching

Strengths
- Numerous aspects of the coaching process captured

Limitations
- Limited inferences that can be made
- Difficult to capture all aspects of the coaching process through a survey
- Social desirability may have played a role

Categories: T2, I, C32, P21

∗ ∗ ∗

Linley, P. A., Woolston, L., & Biswas-Diener, R. (2009). Strengths coaching with leaders. *International Coaching Psychology Review, 4*(1), 37–48.

Relevant Sections: Coaching Process

Purpose
- Demonstrate practice and effects of positive psychology approach to coaching

Design / Methodology
- Discusses CAPP's (Centre for Applied Positive Psychology) Realise2 Model, which identifies strengths; differentiates between strengths, behaviors, and weaknesses; and provides methodologies for applications of strengths

Findings / Implications
- Explicit that leaders identify weaknesses and make them irrelevant
- Encourages leaders to find their optimal balance in using their strengths

Originality / Value
- Employs strengths-based approach to coaching using case studies to illustrate the practice

Strengths
- Provides a historical overview of strengths-based approaches
- Defines strength and introduces alternative strength measures: Clifton Strengths Finder, VIA Inventory of Strengths, Inspirational Leadership Tool

Limitations
- No empirical data to support the effectiveness of strengths coaching

Categories: T1, C31, P12

* * *

Lowman, R. L. (2005). Executive coaching: The road to dodoville needs paving with more than good assumptions. *Consulting Psychology Journal: Practice and Research, 57,* **90–96.**

Relevant Sections: Overview

Purpose
- Review articles from a special executive coaching issue of *The Consulting Psychology Journal: Practice and Research*
- Discuss common themes raised in the executive coaching issue and directions for future research

Design / Methodology
- 10 articles were reviewed from the two-part special issue on executive coaching, published by *The Consulting Psychology Journal: Practice and Research* in winter 2005

Findings / Implications
- Many of the common practices and case studies in the literature lack a scientific foundation
- Trust, environmental context, and coaching model are all identified as vital factors in the executive coaching process
- Characteristics of effective executive coaching include:

      ○ Increased coachee understanding
      ○ A focus on strengths (as opposed to weaknesses)
      ○ The integration of psychological and organizational practices
      ○ Spanning individual, group, and organizational levels
- Future research should combine the information from applied practices with scientifically rigorous methods of psychology

Originality / Value
- Identifies the benefits that both empirical research and applied practices bring to knowledge of executive coaching

Strengths
- Encourages collaboration between practitioners and psychologists

Limitations
- Lacks specific definition of executive coaching
- Reviews relatively small body of executive coaching

Categories: T3, C16, P7

✳ ✳ ✳

Mallen, M. J., Day, S. X., & Green, M. A. (2003). Online versus face-to-face conversations: An examination of relational and discourse variables. *Psychotherapy: Theory, Research, Practice, Training, 40,* **155–163.**

Relevant Sections: Medium

Purpose
- Examine differences in communication processes between online and face-to-face conversations

Design / Methodology
- 32 pairs ($N = 64$) of undergraduate students were randomly assigned to an online or face-to-face communication condition
- Pairs conversed for 20 to 30 minutes, then completed a survey to assess their satisfaction with the interaction, closeness, self-disclosure, emotional understanding, and depth of processing
- Participants were asked to recall facts from the conversation both immediately following the interaction and 10 to 14 days later

Findings / Implications
- Participants in the face-to-face condition reported significantly more satisfaction, closeness, self-disclosure, emotional understanding, and depth of processing than participants in the online condition

- Participants in the face-to-face condition reported significantly less conflict
- In the online condition, participants with more online experience reported higher levels of closeness compared with participants with little online experience
- Results indicate that participants are more cognitively and interpersonally involved in face-to-face conversations compared to online conversations

Originality / Value
- Research specifically pinpointed some of the ways in which online and face-to-face communication differ

Strengths
- Provides information about the emotional and cognitive processes that exist in any form of communication
- Addresses a number of conversational and relational outcomes

Limitations
- Conversations between participants bear little resemblance to coaching practices
    - o Interactions limited to 30 seconds
    - o Participants simply asked to "get to know each other"

Categories: T2, I, M, C26, P9

✱ ✱ ✱

McDermott, M., Levenson, A., & Newton, S. (2007). What coaching can and cannot do for your organization. *Human Resource Planning, 30,* **30–37.**

Relevant Sections: Coaching Outcomes

Purpose
- Examine how organizations use coaching and the perceived organizational outcomes of coaching engagements

Design / Methodology
- 55 companies were surveyed about their use of coaching and the perceived impact of coaching on the organization
- Respondents included human resource representatives responsible for coaching initiatives
- Companies were multinational, publicly traded companies, and the median number of employees was 34,000

Findings / Implications

- Organizations provide coaching on a regular basis to 24 percent of their CEOs and top management teams and 16 percent of their senior vice presidents and general managers
- Coaching has the greatest impact on improving individual-level outcomes such as individuals' leadership behaviors and performance, as well as developing future leaders
- 57 percent of companies planned to increase the use of coaching, while 2 percent planned to decrease coaching and 41 percent reported no plans to change the amount of coaching provided

Originality / Value

- Provides initial insight into organizations' coaching practices and the perceived outcomes from coaching engagements
- Highlights some of the skepticism that human resource professionals have about the use of coaching

Strengths

- Surveyed a broad range of companies

Limitations

- Relies on perceptions of coaching's impact

Categories: T2, C0, P8

* * *

McKenna, D. D., & Davis, S. L. (2009). Hidden in plain sight: The active ingredients of executive coaching. *Industrial and Organizational Psychology: Perspectives on Science and Practice, 2,* **244–260.**

Relevant Sections: Overview

Purpose

- Examine psychotherapy outcome research for ideas to improve executive coaching practices

Design / Methodology

- Conceptual paper
- Generalized "active ingredients" that have been identified as explaining the most variance in psychotherapy outcomes to executive coaching
    - Client/extratherapeutic factors
        - Clients need to be ready and willing to change; coaches need to increase readiness to change of clients and tap into support networks of clients

○ The relationship
  – Coaches should seek to develop an alliance with clients through goals, tasks, and bonds
○ Expectancy, hope, and placebo effects
  – Coaches need to build perceptions of credibility in order to increase client hope
○ Theory and techniques
  – A coach can use theory and techniques to improve or weaken the influence of other active ingredients
  – Coaches should draw on their unique expertise and be clear about how the coaching process will work

Findings / Implications
- Psychotherapy findings argued to inform executive coaching
- Active ingredients are interactive; they blend together and influence other factors
- Executive coaching and psychotherapy differ in important ways

Originality / Value
- Interesting connection between the executive coaching and psychotherapy literatures

Strengths
- Empirical research and additional rationale needed to support the relevance of all factors to executive coaching

Limitations: None noted

Categories: T1, I, C33, P17

✳ ✳ ✳

Nowack, K. M. (2009). Leveraging multirater feedback to facilitate successful behavioral change. *Consulting Psychology Journal: Practice and Research, 61*(4)**, 280–297.**

Relevant Sections: Coaching Process

Purpose
- Present a three-stage model for behavior change to increase the impact of multirater feedback

Design / Methodology
- Conceptual article that proposes a three-stage model of behavior change:
  1. Enlighten: 360-degree feedback, readiness to change, motivational interviewing

2. Encourage: goal definition, goal setting, skill building
3. Enable: reinforcement, monitoring, building in social support, relapse prevention training, evaluation

Findings / Implications
- 360-degree feedback is a common component of many coaching programs, yet there are many limitations
  - o Scores between rater groups (e.g., peers, subordinates) are only modestly correlated
  - o Scores within rater groups (e.g., between two peers) are only modestly correlated
- Feedback combined with coaching can increase clients' performance

Originality / Value
- Examines weaknesses of multirater feedback and provides model to help overcome these weaknesses

Strengths
- Provides foundation for successfully incorporating multirater feedback into coaching programs

Limitations
- Model needs empirical support

Categories: T1, C78, P18

✳ ✳ ✳

O'Broin, A., & Palmer, S. (2006). The coach-client relationship and contributions made by the coach in improving coaching outcome. *The Coaching Psychologist, 2*(2), 16–20.

Relevant Sections: Coach-Client Matching, Coaching Process

Purpose
- Advocate research focusing on the coach-client relationship

Design / Methodology
- Reviews the coaching literature to support arguments for the need and direction of coach-client relationship research

Findings / Implications
- Discusses coaching relationship themes within current coaching literature
  - o Coaching relationship is seen as a tool of change
  - o Exploration of credentials for effective coaching
  - o Coaching occurs in stages

- Promotes applying the principle of best current knowledge, borrowing from allied fields
- Psychotherapy Task Force (Lambert & Barley, 2001) identified three factors influencing outcomes:
    1. Therapist variables (interpersonal style, therapist attributes)
    2. Facilitative conditions (empathy, warmth, congruence)
    3. Therapeutic alliance (tasks, bonds and goals)

Originality / Value
- Currently, the only literature review that focuses on the coach-client relationship

Strengths
- Presents a salient discussion of issues relevant to coach-client relationships
- Offers a series of coach-client questions to guide future research
    - What are the perceptions of both clients and coaches on the relationship?
    - How is the coaching relationship related to coaching outcomes?
    - Can coach contributions improve the coach-client relationship?
    - Can the coach-client relationship be effectively tailored to the individual client?

Limitations
- Minimal evidence or guidance to support answering the questions proposed

Categories: T3, I, C43, P5

$* * *$

O'Broin, A., & Palmer, S. (2009). Co-creating an optimal coaching alliance: A cognitive behavioural coaching perspective. *International Coaching Psychology Review, 4*(2), 184–194.

Relevant Sections: Coaching Process, Coach-Client Matching

Purpose
- Provide a cognitive behavioral perspective to support coaching relationships

Design / Methodology
- Examines coach-client relationships from a cognitive behavioral perspective with support by research from counseling and psychotherapy literature

Findings / Implications
- Coaching alliance characterized by explicitly agreed-upon goals, tasks, bonds, and views helps create trust and respect in the coaching relationship
- Work-supporting bonds linking goals and tasks may be more instructive than coach-client bonds (coach empathy, genuineness, and unconditional acceptance of client) to collaborative relationship
- Empathy enables cognitive behavior processes and therefore is proposed as a key coaching relationship factor
- Coaching bond is enhanced when a good match exists between coach and client interpersonal styles, particularly in the early stages of establishing coaching alliance

Originality / Value
- Emphasizes collaborative nature of a coach-client relationship and provides an approach to developing a coaching alliance
- Highlights psychological or coaching contracts that are based on schemas, promises, and mutuality as a tool in developing effective collaborative relationships

Strengths
- Defines cognitive behavioral coaching
- Provides a cognitive behavioral therapy context, indicating evidence-based research support

Limitations
- No empirical data to support the effectiveness of cognitive behavioral coaching

Categories: T1, C65, P11

***

Orenstein, R. (2002). Executive coaching: It's not just about the executive. *Journal of Applied Behavioral Science, 38,* **355–374.**

Relevant Sections: Overview, Organizational Support

Purpose
- Challenge the conventional notion that executive coaching is an individual-level intervention

Design / Methodology
- Draws on academic literature, applied practices, and the author's experiences

- Provides four premises for the executive coaching process and three illustrative examples of when and how these premises apply

Findings / Implications
- Current literature defines executive coaching as "a one-on-one intervention with a senior manager for the purpose of improving or enhancing management skills" (p. 356)
- The literature, while limited, demonstrates the success of coaching practices that emphasize the individual as part of a greater system
- To understand the higher-level relationship, four premises should guide coaching behaviors:
    1. A focus on the unconscious
    2. Consideration of the individual, the organization, and their interaction
    3. The multilevel relationship between the individual and the group
    4. Use of the self

Originality / Value
- Provides clear agenda for integrating the organization into coaching interventions
- Provides illustrations of when and how to apply the agenda

Strengths
- Emphasis on the role of the organizational system in executive coaching

Limitations
- Does not fully differentiate between coaching and therapy

Categories: T1, I, C37, P20

✳ ✳ ✳

Orenstein, R. L. (2006). Measuring executive coaching efficacy? The answer was right here all the time. *Consulting Psychology Journal: Practice and Research, 58,* **106–116.**

Relevant Sections: Coaching Outcomes

Purpose
- Examine a survey approach for assessing the effectiveness of coaching engagements
- The Empathic Organic Questionnaire (Alderfer & Brown, 1972) was applied to coaching by adapting the questions to focus on individual change within an organizational role

Design / Methodology
- Examined one executive that the author worked with as a coach over a period of six months
- 20 members of the organization rated the client's behavior on a variety of dimensions before and after the coaching engagement
- Assessment dimensions included behaviors that were directly related to the coaching engagement, behaviors that were indirectly related to the coaching engagement, and control items that were unrelated to the coaching engagement
- Used *t*-tests to compare the ratings of the client's behavior before and after coaching

Findings / Implications
- Ratings of client's behaviors directly related to the coaching objectives showed the most number of significant changes before and after the coaching engagement (79 percent)
- 9 percent of behaviors indirectly related to the coaching objectives were significantly rated as changing and none of the control items were significantly rated as changing

Originality / Value
- Findings suggest that relevant others in the organization could diagnose the behavioral changes targeted by the coaching intervention

Strengths
- Provides a description of one technique that organizations can use to evaluate the outcomes of coaching engagements

Limitations
- Small sample size (only examined one client)

Categories: T4, C18, P11

***

Passmore, J. (2007). An integrative model for executive coaching. *Consulting Psychology Journal: Practice and Research, 59*(1), 68–78.

Relevant Sections: Coaching Process

Purpose
- Bring together a series of evidence-based coaching approaches to build an integrated model for executive coaching

Design / Methodology
- The Integrative Coaching Model is presented and its elements described

Findings / Implications

- The Integrative Coaching Model consists of six streams:
    1. Developing the coaching partnership draws from the humanistic tradition
    2. Maintaining the coaching partnership draws from both emotional intelligence and the psychoanalytic tradition
    3. Behavioral focus draws from behaviorism and is at the core of all executive coaching
    4. Conscious cognition draws upon cognitive-behavioral interventions
    5. Unconscious cognition focuses on cognitive processes outside of conscious awareness and draws from the psychoanalytic tradition
    6. Cultural context in which coach and coachee operate
- Developing and maintaining a coaching partnership is critical but insufficient
- To move toward enhanced performance, the executive coach must work in four streams of change:
    1. What they can see — the behavioral
    2. What they can't see but rather hear from the cognitive processes at work
    3. What they suspect, at the unconscious level
    4. Within the system by which the coachee is bound

Originality / Value

- The model provides executive coaches with a starting point from which to practice, reflect on, and develop further
- Offers an eclectic way to coach, mixing tools and techniques from various approaches
- Model uses the concept of working at multiple levels — behavioral, cognitive, and unconscious
- Acknowledges that although the integrative model is not unique, the blend of elements is a distinctive approach

Strengths

- Model is heavily evidence-based
- Serves to provide a holistic model of executive coaching that can be used as a guide in the business world

Limitations: None noted

Categories: T1, C45, P12

✳ ✳ ✳

Passmore, J., & Gibbes, C. (2007). The state of executive coaching research: What does the current literature tell us and what's next for coaching research? *International Coaching Psychology Review, 2,* **116–128.**

Relevant Sections: Overview

Purpose
- Review past research from executive coaching studies, coaching case studies, life coaching practices, and counseling psychology in order to integrate and assess the extant literature

Design / Methodology
- Reviews executive coaching literature, field studies, survey studies, life coaching studies, and counseling psychology literature
- Literature search was restricted to studies published after 2000

Findings / Implications
- Case and survey studies show promising results about the efficacy of executive coaching
- Small body of empirical research highlights important inputs and moderators such as:
  - Leader behaviors
  - Ratings
  - Credibility
  - Coachee perceptions
- Counseling psychology literature contains more expansive and definitive research that empirically validates practices and outcomes
  - Possible methods and pathways from counseling psychology research can be used to further validate executive coaching hypotheses

Originality / Value
- Consolidated review of recent executive coaching literature

Strengths
- Integrates findings from wide array of areas

Limitations
- No clear definition of executive coaching
- Little differentiation between coaching and counseling

Categories: T3, I, C65, P13

* * *

Passmore, J., Rawle-Cope, M., Gibbes, C., & Holloway, M. (2006). MBTI® types and executive coaching. *The Coaching Psychologist,* 2(3), 6–14.

Relevant Sections: Coach-Client Matching, Coach and Client Characteristics

Purpose
- Examine personality preferences of executive coaches as indicated by MBTI

Design / Methodology
- 228 experienced executive coaches completed an online survey (15 percent completion rate)
  - Four MBTI type preferences
  - Psychological training
  - Preferred methodology from 12 approaches (e.g., humanistic, cognitive, behavioral, integrated, psychodynamic, solution focused)
- Data analyzed by the four preferences and 12 MBTI types (e.g., ISTJ)

Findings / Implications
- U.K. coaches versus U.K. populations
  - ISFJ: 0.9 percent of U.K. coaches (13 percent of U.K. population)
  - ENFP: 18.9 percent of U.K. coaches (6 percent of U.K. population)
  - Extraversion (E): 57.4 percent of U.K. coaches (53 percent of U.K. population)
  - Intuition (N): 84.2 percent of U.K. coaches (17 percent of U.K. population)
  - Perceiving (P): 53.5 percent of U.K. coaches (41 percent of U.K. population)
- Coaches more concerned with big picture rather than a detailed approach (S/N)
- Also examined differences between psychologist and nonpsychologist coaches
  - Intuition (N): 89.9 percent psychologists (81.2 percent of nonpsychologists)
  - Feeling (F): 47.7 percent of psychologists (52.2 percent of nonpsychologists)
  - Perhaps a result of training offered or types attracted to be psychologists

Originality / Value
- Discusses need for coaches to understand how their personality type may affect interaction with clients
- Presents likely strengths and areas for development for coaches (e.g., MBTI: "F"; Strength: "Being empathetic"; Development: "Challenging the coachee" (p. 13; Table 8)

Strengths
- Defines "experienced coach" as more than "50 hours of executive coaching" (p. 6)
- Presents a general overview of MBTI
- Good integration of the counseling literature

Limitations
- Participants were self-selected (19.2 percent of 1,500 invited to participate)
- Article focused on a subset of variables from a larger study exploring coaching behaviors, which were not discussed

Categories: T2, C8, P9

∗ ∗ ∗

Perkins, R. D. (2009). How executive coaching can change leader behavior and improve meeting effectiveness: An exploratory study. *Consulting Psychology Journal: Practice and Research, 61*(4), 298–318.

Relevant Sections: Coaching Process

Purpose
- Describe a coaching process and information on how executive coaching can help executives improve *meeting leadership*

Design / Methodology
- An exploratory study designed to answer the following questions:
  - Can more effective meeting behaviors be identified?
  - Can the identified behaviors be changed through executive coaching?
  - Will behavioral changes lead to positive individual and organizational outcomes?
- Participants were 21 executives (20 men, 1 woman)
- The Meeting Leadership Measurement System (MLMS) was developed to assess leaders' meeting behaviors pre- and post-coaching

and included asking questions, summarizing, testing for consensus, disagreeing, attacking, and giving information
- Three cases are presented to demonstrate how coaching was done using the MLMS

Findings / Implications
- After coaching, participants demonstrated significant behavioral changes
- Coached behavioral changes led to increased understanding and improved skills in meeting leadership, and more positive meeting outcomes
- Productive meeting leadership behaviors can be identified and changed with executive coaching that utilizes positively framed, objective feedback

Originality / Value
- The MLMS may offer executives concrete performance data as valuable feedback on their development and a means to document specific improvements in leadership effectiveness as a result of executive coaching
- Advances the business meeting literature, a typically ignored yet ubiquitous and very important component of the executive role

Strengths
- Provides a valid coding system to tally behavioral categories, which makes collecting data about executive coaching possible and provides a way for practitioners to document their results and share insights

Limitations
- The study sample consists almost entirely of white, male, well-educated, and successful executives, limiting the generalizability of the study results
- Potential for rater bias in coding

Categories: T2 & T4, M, C46, P20

✳ ✳ ✳

Pulley, M. L. (2006). Blended coaching. In S. Ting & P. Scisco (Eds.), *The Center for Creative Leadership handbook of coaching* **(pp. 347–378). San Francisco, CA: John Wiley & Sons.**

Relevant Sections: Medium

Purpose
- Examine supplementing traditional face-to-face coaching with other modalities

Design / Methodology
- Interviewed professional coaches to gain insight regarding blended coaching

Findings / Implications
- Describes a variety of distance modalities in terms of synchronous and asynchronous communication
  - Synchronous: telephone, audiovideo conferencing, webcam, text chat/IM
  - Asynchronous: e-mail, online assessments, threaded discussion, peer-to-peer collaborative platforms, Web-enabled follow-up processes
  - Skill-building: webinar, archived audio/video, online resources
- Characteristics that distinguish distance modalities from face-to-face: technology, lack of nonverbal cues, importance of clarity, confidentiality
- Issues to consider when designing blended coaching experiences include
  - Assessing coach's readiness
  - Assessing client readiness
  - Sustaining the relationship over time and distance
  - What to blend
- Three case examples of blended coaching are provided to illustrate these four issues

Originality / Value
- Describes pros and cons of distance modalities
- Discusses issues to consider when assessing both the coach and client readiness for blended coaching
- Offers a list of coaching skills specific to blended coaching (Exhibit 13.1)

Strengths
- Provides detailed cases of blended coaching within CCL's coaching framework

Limitations
- Limited discussion regarding the future possibilities of blended coaching

Categories: T4 & T5, C9, P32

∗ ∗ ∗

Quick, J. C., & Macik-Frey, M. (2004). Behind the mask: Coaching through deep interpersonal communication. *Consulting Psychology Journal: Practice and Research, 56*(2), 67–74.

Relevant Sections: Coaching Process

Purpose
- Executive coaching through deep interpersonal communication is discussed as a vehicle for executive development and enhancing the individual's and organization's health

Design / Methodology
- Developed a health-enhancing developmental model based on the two authors' professional experience with executives, military officers, and university presidents

Findings / Implications
- An interpersonal approach focused on safe, secure communication in which difficult, complicated issues are addressed and critical conversations occur
- A two-tiered model of executive communication is proposed:
    1. In the outer tier the executive engages in functional, organizational communication via a variety of mediums
    2. In the inner tier the executive engages in much more personal and intimate communication
- The deep interpersonal level is where the executive is truly authentic and must deal with inner conflict and tension
- Multiple positive outcomes are suggested as a result of using deep interpersonal communication:
    o Health benefits such as reducing stress and pressure
    o Health of the organization by influencing work climate and employee morale
- Role of the executive coach is to enable the authentic person that is in every executive to become an authentic leader

Originality / Value
- Works from the premise that to develop fully and grow healthy, executives must work and live with character and a deep sense of personal integrity
- In sync with positive psychology emphasizing building on individual strengths rather than correcting shortcomings and limitations
- Emphasizes the importance of authenticity, integrity, and relationships for leadership effectiveness in executives

Strengths
- Thought-provoking article providing a unique perspective on the role of executives and executive coaches

Limitations
- Specific methods and techniques are not provided

Categories: T1, C31, P8

✳ ✳ ✳

Renner, J. C. (2007). Coaching abroad: Insights about assets. *Consulting Psychology Journal: Practice and Research, 59*(4), 272–285.

Relevant Sections: Coach and Client Characteristics, Coaching Process

Purpose
- Explore the rationale and method for coaching noncorporate managers

Design / Methodology
- Conceptual discussion supported with examples of issues to consider when coaching in less developed countries (LDCs) and in smaller companies in developed countries (DCs)
- Arguments intend to support using Asset Management Model in LDC coaching

Findings / Implications
- Leadership competency issues are examined in terms of transportability and cultural differences
    - Western leadership competencies may not be appropriate in LDCs; therefore coaches need to engage managers in a discussion about "what works"
    - For example, "Ambition, competitiveness, fear of poverty, limited opportunities for advancement mean that coaching managers in LDCs requires an understanding of survival tactics" (p. 274)

      o Autocratic managers perceived as more effective in many poorer countries
- Lists seven working conditions that differ in LCDs based on personal experience
- Asset Management Model in Coaching
  - o Focus: (1) Level of ambition, (2) Asset acquisition successes, and (3) Creative ideas for using assets
  - o Employs five-step process before identifying targets for change
  - o Few situations in LDCs use multirater surveys

Originality / Value
- Addresses the challenge of coaching managers abroad with no or little experience working for global corporations and little management training

Strengths
- Integrates personal examples to illustrate international coaching experiences
- Includes additional references to illustrate and support personal examples

Limitations
- Examples presented were not necessarily focused on coaching

Categories: T5, C27, P14

✳ ✳ ✳

Riddle, D., Zan, L., & Kuzmycz, D. (2009). Five myths about executive coaching. *Leadership in Action, 29*(5), 19–21.

Relevant Sections: Coach-Client Matching, Coaching Process

Purpose
- Provide a brief overview of executive coaching myths with the goal of highlighting ways the coaching community can establish industry standards and regulations to improve coaching effectiveness

Design / Methodology
- Article presents five coaching myths:
  1. Coaching credentials mean coaching effectiveness
  2. There's a magical philosophy or approach to coaching
  3. It's all about the coach
  4. The best coaches sat in that hot seat
  5. You're going to love my coach

Findings / Implications
- Coaching credentials should be viewed in conjunction with other factors (e.g., references) when selecting a coach
- The key to effective coaching is not a trademarked process but rather a variety of factors including the coach's background, the coach-client match, and the management of the coaching relationship
- There may not be an ideal set of coach characteristics; the relationship between the coach and client is more important than a particular set of coach characteristics
- The coach's ability to help the client meet his or her needs is more important than the coach's experience or background
- No coach is right for every client

Originality / Value
- Provides ideas for directions the field can go in to move past these misconceptions about coaching

Strengths
- Provides concise overview of some of the misconceptions of coaching and provides direction for moving the field past these misconceptions

Limitations
- Limited information presented for each of the myths

Categories: T1, C0, P3

* * *

Scoular, A., & Linley, P. A. (2006). Coaching, goal-setting and personality type: What matters? *The Coaching Psychologist, 2*(1), 9–11.

Relevant Sections: Coach-Client Matching

Purpose
- Examine how best to match coaches and clients

Design / Methodology
- Experimental design
  - 120 30-minute coaching sessions (first meeting)
  - 14 experienced coaches and clients from eight U.K. organizations matched randomly
  - 60 sessions used goal setting; 60 sessions did not use goal setting
- Coach and client completed
  - MBTI & NEO personality questionnaires

      o An "evaluation questionnaire" at the end of session, 2 and 8 weeks)

      o Qualitative feedback where clients listed specific outcomes achieved from session

Findings / Implications

- No significant difference between goal-setting and non-goal-setting conditions
- Differences in coach and client MBTI temperaments resulted in higher outcome scores

Originality / Value

- Findings suggest that in matches differing on temperament, "the coach may instinctively come for a different perspective and perhaps challenge" clients' assumptions more and that the more complex interaction leads to higher performance outcomes (p. 11)

Strengths

- Provides evidence to support matching client and coaches on differences on personality temperaments (MBTI)

Limitations

- No details regarding the research study's design participant characteristics (e.g., gender, age), measures, analyses, or statistical results
- No manipulation check; coach feedback suggested alternative means of goal setting may have occurred during non-goal-setting session; coaches compensated or altered coaching to ensure session beneficial
- Didn't discuss examination of stated hypothesis, "Did similarity of personality lead to better communication or did difference lead to useful change?"

Categories: T2 & T5, C13, P3

✳ ✳ ✳

Sherin, J., & Caiger, L. (2004). Rational-emotive behavior therapy: A behavioral change model for executive coaching? *Consulting Psychology Journal: Practice and Research, 56*(4), 225–233.

Relevant Sections: Coaching Process

Purpose

- Review the rational-emotive behavior therapy (REBT) process
- Discuss its applicability in the context of a coaching relationship in which the focus is executive performance

Design / Methodology

- A theoretical perspective of executive coaching based on REBT as a behavioral change model

Findings / Implications

- Client's explicit and implicit belief system is seen as the locus of change
- Coach works with clients to identify and dispute unreasonable expectations that negatively impact performance
- Rational-emotive behavior coaching (REBC) can be applied to various issues that impede an executive's performance such as perfectionism, anger management, and low frustration tolerance
- Most obvious advantage of REBC is its targeted nature
  - o Short-term intervention most appropriate when dealing with discrete issues
  - o Works to increase client's capacity for rational, critical, and psychologically sophisticated reasoning
  - o Subsequent benefit is the reduction of mental rigidity and increased flexible thinking
- The ABCDE model of individual change is applied to coaching: Activating event, Belief, Consequences, Disputing problematic beliefs, Effective outlook

Originality / Value

- Provides coaches seeking different interventions with options for integrating certain techniques into their existing models of change

Strengths

- Provides specific, concrete steps that walk the reader through REBC
- Explicitly identifies which coaching situations are appropriate for REBC

Limitations

- Does not address the disadvantages of REBC and when it may be a less appropriate coaching intervention

Categories: T1, C42, P9

***

Smither, J., London, M., Flautt, R., Vargas, Y., & Kucine, I. (2003). Can working with an executive coach improve multisource feedback ratings over time? A quasi-experimental field study. *Personnel Psychology, 56,* **23–44.**

Relevant Sections: Outcomes

Purpose
- Examine the effects of coaching on multisource feedback over time

Design / Methodology
- Quasi-empirical study
- Utilized a pre/post design with a control group
- Participants included 404 senior managers who received coaching and 957 managers who did not
- All participants received multisource feedback over a one-year period.

Findings / Implications
- Compared with managers who did not engage in coaching, participants who worked with a coach improved more in terms of direct report and supervisor ratings ($d = .17$).
- Compared with the control group, participants who worked with a coach were more likely to set specific goals ($d = .16$) and to solicit ideas for improvement from their supervisors ($d = .36$)

Originality / Value
- Article provides an empirical evaluation of the effects of coaching on multisource ratings

Strengths
- Pre/post design
- Includes multisource data
- Large sample size

Limitations
- Multisource ratings were also shared with clients' supervisor, which may have decreased the incremental gain from working with a coach

Categories: T2, M, C41, P21

* * *

Sparrow, S. (2008). Finding a coach: The perfect match. *Training and Coaching Today.* **Retrieved November 16, 2008, from http://www. personneltoday.com/articles/2008/01/22/43943/finding-a-coach-the-perfect-match.html**

Relevant Sections: Coach-Client Matching

Purpose
- Examine what facilitates the "perfect coaching relationship"

Design / Methodology
- 200 managers selected three potential coaches by
  - Examining coach biographies (photo, qualifications, philosophy, experience)
  - Contacting the potential coaches (e-mail, phone, face-to-face meeting)

Findings / Implications
- Clients based decisions on subjective criteria: instinct and empathy
  - Empathy defined as "similarity of outlook"
  - Qualitative data indicated female coaches preferred by both sexes
    – Females felt female coaches were good role models
    – Males felt female coaches were better for discussing personal issues
  - Quantitative analysis provided no evidence of gender preference
- Recommendations from research
  - Suggests offering choice with transparency
  - Employ psychometric testing with follow-up to ensure rapport
- Opinions of expert practitioners
  - Focus on coach's skills, not personality or character match
  - Personal chemistry can't be measured; focus on philosophy match
    – Focus on mutual values, similar ideas about development and learning
    – Consider the specific coaching objectives and the match to organization
  - Include a "chemistry" meeting
  - Match on personality characteristics
  - Provide client choices in coaches

Originality / Value
- Recommends a "key objective" for those charged with arranging coaching to ensure coach and clients are "well-matched"
- Demonstrates conflicting views on client-coach matching criteria

Strengths
- Includes several perspectives from seven diverse organizations

Limitations
- No details regarding the research study's design, analyses, or statistical results
- No support for claims (e.g., "a mismatch costs more and potentially can do a lot of damage to people and organizations")

Categories: T1 & T5, C0, P6

* * *

Stern, L. (2004). Executive coaching: A working definition. *Consulting Psychology Journal: Practice and Research, 56,* **154–162.**

Relevant Sections: Overview

Purpose
- Propose working definition of "executive coaching," and how it differs from other coaching practices
- Outline examples of executive coaching applications, competencies required of executive coaches, and steps for coach development

Design / Methodology
- Draws from academic journals, practice journals, and the author's own experience

Findings / Implications
- Defines executive coaching as a unique, personalized partnership between coach and leader, in which the primary focus is to develop skills and competencies within the leader
  - Geared toward fostering the goals of the organization
- Multilevel approach is what most differentiates executive coaching from other practices such as career, personal, or team coaching
- Executive coaching can satisfy a multitude of organizational needs, including executive development and assessment, performance management, strategy building, team building, conflict resolution, and change management

- Characteristics and developmental steps for executive coaches:
  - o Expertise in both business and psychology
  - o Depending on client needs, must be knowledgeable in other areas (e.g., stress management, labor relations, or work-life balance)
  - o Provide concrete ideas, solutions, and feedback that are specifically tailored to the organization, industry, and executive
  - o Actively continue their own development in order to meet practice needs
- When seeking executive coaches, organizations should consider the coach's knowledge of business, specific skills and expertise, familiarity with the industry, and personal chemistry with the executive

Originality / Value

- Offers a comprehensive definition of executive coaching as a starting point to consolidating and advancing research and practices

Strengths

- Outlines concrete steps for furthering executive coaching practice and research

Limitations

- Draws on limited body of empirical research

Categories: T1, I, C11, P9

✳ ✳ ✳

Stevens, J. H., Jr. (2005). Executive coaching from the executive's perspective. *Consulting Psychology Journal: Practice and Research, 57*(4), 274–285.

Relevant Sections: Coach and Client Characteristics

Purpose

- Examine views and beliefs related to executive coaching held by top executives

Design / Methodology

- Informal interviews conducted by author with seven top management executives who had participated in executive coaching
- 11 preconstructed questions used as the basis for the conversation

Findings / Implications

- Executives sought coaching to have their thinking challenged and to receive help increasing clarity and objectivity in their thinking

- Coaches valued for their ability to provide a detached perspective
- Characteristics of coaches perceived to be important
    - Intelligence
    - Experience with pressures and responsibilities executives face
    - Listening skills
    - Sincere interest in the coaching relationship
    - Demeanor
    - Formal training not considered as important as skills and knowledge related to people dynamics and organizational dynamics
- Coaching provided opportunity for reflection
- Confidentiality viewed as critical in the coaching process
- Coaching a unique process for each individual
- Confidentiality perceived as more easily achieved with external coaches

Originality / Value
- Examines executive coaching from the perspective of the coachee

Strengths
- Coachee perspective of the coaching process

Limitations
- Limited sample; limited generalizability
- Preconstructed questions may have influenced the themes that were observed

Categories: T4, C16, P11

✳ ✳ ✳

Stewart, L. J., Palmer, S., Wilkin, H., & Kerrin, M. (2008). The influence of character: Does personality impact coaching success? *International Journal of Evidence Based Coaching and Mentoring, 6*(1), 32–42.

Relevant Sections: Coach and Client Characteristics, Coach-Client Matching

Purpose
- Examine the relationship between clients' personalities and transfer of learning from executive coaching to the workplace

Design / Methodology
- Convenience sample recruited via e-mail ($n = 100$; 60 male/40 female)
- Self-report data: personality and coaching transfer
    - International Personality Item Pool (IPIP, 3 subscales/30 items; Goldberg, 1999)

- o General Perceived Self-Efficacy Scale (10 items; Schwarzer & Jerusalem, 1993)
- o Coaching Transfer Questionnaire (CTQ, 24 items; Stewart, 2006, master's thesis)

Findings / Implications

- Personality measures may be minimally useful for identifying successful clients
  - o Conscientiousness, openness to experience, emotional stability, general self-efficacy correlate with CTQ Application subscale ($r = .28, .24, -.21, .22, p < .05$, respectively)
  - o Conscientiousness correlated with CTQ Generalization and Maintenance subscale ($r = .22, p < .05$)

Originality / Value

- Responds to organizational concerns regarding selecting coaching candidates
- Suggests certain personalities may benefit from organization providing transfer support

Strengths

- Provides support to coaching literature that is generally consistent with personality and training studies
- Includes categories for client participation in coaching (i.e., accelerate career development, gain career direction clarity, advice of senior, prepare for upcoming challenge, volunteer/nonvolunteer)

Limitations

- Reflects coaching success and coaching transfer as separate outcomes
- Does not focus on traditional coaching outcomes, instead adapting Schmitt et al.'s (2003) model of employee performance
- Magnitude of correlations effect size relatively low

Categories: T2, C35, P10

* * *

Sue-Chan, S., & Latham, G. P. (2004). The relative effectiveness of external, peer, and self-coaches. *Applied Psychology: An International Review, 53*(2), 260–278.

Relevant Sections: Coach and Client Characteristics

Purpose

- Evaluate effectiveness of coaching as influenced by whether coaching is provided by self, a peer, or an external individual

Design / Methodology
- Study One
    - Sample: First-semester North American MBA students
    - $N = 30$
    - Assigned to one of three coaching conditions
        – Source of coaching: self, peer, or external
- Study Two
    - Sample: Experienced Australian managers enrolled in EMBA program
    - $N = 23$
    - Assigned to one of three coaching conditions
        – Source of coaching: self, peer, or external

Findings / Implications
- Study One
    - External and peer coaches appeared satisfied with training on how to conduct a coaching session
    - Coaching from an external individual resulted in higher performance than coaching from a peer
    - External coaches were perceived as more credible than peer or self coaches
- Study Two
    - Managers coached by an external coach or self-coached received a higher course grade than those coached by a peer
    - External coaches were perceived as more credible than peer coaches
    - Individuals coached by an external coach were more satisfied with coaching sessions than those in the self- or peer-coaching conditions

Originality / Value
- Examines impact of the source of coaching

Strengths
- Provides comparison of different sources of coaching

Limitations
- Coaching from different sources in organizational work settings needed in future research
- Coaching skills in each condition may not have been equivalent
- Research needs to investigate why coaching sources may have differed in effectiveness
- Limited generalizability

Categories: T2, I, M, C60, P19

***

Thach, E. (2002). The impact of executive coaching and 360 feedback on leadership effectiveness. *Leadership and Organization Development Journal, 23,* **205–214.**

Relevant Sections: Coaching Outcomes

Purpose
- Examine the effects of coaching and 360-degree feedback on perceptions of leadership competency

Design / Methodology
- 281 executives and high-potential managers at a midsize telecommunications company
- Study included three phases conducted over almost three years
  - Phase one—the 360-degree survey was designed and piloted on 57 executives
  - Phase two—the 360-degree survey was used for 168 executives; each executive also received a one-hour debrief coaching session on the results of the 360-degree survey as well as three additional coaching sessions over the next six months
  - After the completion of the coaching sessions, 360-degree surveys were again distributed to the participants' peers, direct reports, and managers
  - Phase three—identical to the second phase with another 113 executives

Findings / Implications
- Overall effect of 360-degree feedback and coaching showed an average increase in perceived leadership effectiveness of 55 percent for executives in phase two and 60 percent for executives in phase three

Originality / Value
- Findings support the positive effects of coaching and 360-degree feedback on perceived leadership effectiveness

Strengths
- Pre/post design
- Includes multisource data
- Large sample size

Limitations
- Coaching and 360-degree feedback were provided as package intervention; difficult to determine if effects were from coaching, 360-degree feedback, or both

Categories: T2, M, C31, P10

✳ ✳ ✳

Ting, S., & Hart, E. W. (2003). Formal coaching. In C. D. McCauley & E. Van Velsor (Eds.), *The Center for Creative Leadership handbook of leadership development* **(2nd ed., pp. 116–150). San Francisco, CA: Jossey-Bass.**

Relevant Sections: Overview, Coach and Client Characteristics, Coach-Client Matching, Coaching Process, Organizational Support

Purpose
- Review the Center for Creative Leadership's practice of formal executive coaching for the purpose of leader development

Design / Methodology
- Review article providing a framework for understanding factors of the formal coaching process

Findings / Implications
- Coaching was defined as "a practice in which the coachee and the coach collaborate to assess and understand the coachee and his or her developmental task, to challenge current constraints while exploring new possibilities to ensure accountability and support for reaching goals and sustaining development" (p. 116)
- Three aspects of coaching process
  - Relationship
    - Importance of rapport, collaboration, and commitment
    - Argued relationship serves as vehicle supporting ACS
  - Assessment, challenge, and support (ACS)
    - Assessment facilitates self-awareness of the coachee
    - Challenge creates a state of disequilibrium
    - Support should help the coachees "right" themselves following challenge
  - Results
    - Results should focus on behavioral change, personal development, and learning agility
    - Multiple sources provide more complete view of the coachee's accomplishments.
- Principles forming the foundation for coaching
  - Safe but challenging environment
  - Work with the coachee's agenda
  - Facilitate
  - Advocate self-awareness
  - Promote sustainable learning from experience
  - Model what is coached

- Three phases of the coaching process
  - Preprogram activities (needs and readiness assessment; matching of coach and client)
    - Important client characteristics
      - Individual readiness
      - Psychological readiness
      - Environmental readiness
    - Factors important in matching coach and coachee
      - Compatibility in behavioral preferences, personality, interpersonal needs, and work style
      - Similar interests and background (personal, educational, and work)
      - Similar work experience
  - Program implementation activities
    - Building the coach-coachee relationship
    - Coming to a shared understanding of the coaching process
    - Assessing current state of the coachee
    - Reviewing feedback
    - Forming and implementing a learning agenda
  - Postprogram activities
    - Evaluating the program and coach effectiveness

Originality / Value

- Framework for understanding important factors of the coaching process

Strengths

- Numerous factors of the coaching process considered
- Clear definitions of aspects of the coaching process

Limitations

- Exclusive focus on the Center for Creative Leadership coaching perspective

Categories: T3, I, C0, P34

* * *

Turner, R. A., & Goodrich, J. (2010). The case for eclecticism in executive coaching: Application to challenging assignments. *Consulting Psychology Journal: Practice and Research, 62*(1), 39–55.

Relevant Sections: Coaching Process

Purpose

- Describe a coaching process for high-achieving executives around performance problems related to emotion management in interpersonal work interactions

Design / Methodology

- A discussion of two case studies in which the following are addressed:
  - o Circumstances of leaders who lose control of their usually polished demeanor
  - o Typical characteristics of leaders with emotional experience and expression problems
  - o How problems come to the attention of the organization and coaches and what different models and approaches are helpful in practice
- The case studies are an amalgamation of cases the authors have worked on and describe overt expressions of anger that have become extremely problematic for the executives

Findings / Implications

- The future of executive coaching will need to be based on multiple theoretical approaches and techniques that can be utilized within the same coaching engagement to guide decision making and interventions at different levels (individual versus interpersonal or group) and at different stages over time
- This is especially the case for long-term, difficult cases and those that have a combination of individual and organizational characteristics that contribute to poor performance; case in point is that of very high performers, highly valuable to the organization, but who manage with a volatile emotional style

Originality / Value

- Integrates different theoretical approaches to executive coaching derived from the larger field of psychology (i.e., psychodynamic, cognitive-behavioral, systems, attribution theories, social learning, and theory of individual differences) in the expressive display of emotion
- Stimulates thinking about how practitioners in psychology use their various psychological skills and knowledge beyond a one- or two-theory solution to enhance change in individuals and groups

Strengths
- Provides strategies for coaching engagements that are particularly difficult

Limitations
- Discussion based only on authors' subjective field experience

Categories: T4, I, C63, P16

$$* * *$$

Wasylyshyn, K. M. (2003). Executive coaching: An outcome study. *Consulting Psychology Journal: Practice and Research, 55,* **94–106.**

Relevant Sections: Overview, Coaching Outcomes

Purpose
- Explore the factors influencing the selection of a coach, preference for coaching tools, and indications of successful coaching engagements

Design / Methodology
- A survey was distributed to 106 executives that the author coached between 1985 and 2001
- The majority of the clients worked at Fortune 500 organizations
- 87 clients completed and returned the survey, an 82 percent response rate

Findings / Implications
- The top credential criteria that clients noted influenced their choice in coaches included graduate training in psychology and business experience—reflecting a need for coaches to be grounded in both business and psychology
- The top personal characteristics that clients identified with an effective coach were the ability to form a strong connection with the client and professionalism
- The top-rated coaching tools were coaching sessions, 360-degree feedback, and relationship with the coach
- The top indicators of successful coaching included sustained behavioral change, increased self-awareness, and more-effective leadership.

Originality / Value
- Provides insight into clients' perspectives as to what factors make an effective coach, what coaching tools are successful, and the indicators of successful coaching

Strengths
- Large sample size

Limitations
- Relies on self-report data from clients

Categories: T2, C9, P13

$$* \, * \, *$$

Wycherley, I. A., & Cox, E. (2008). Factors in the selection and matching of executive coaches in organizations. *Coaching: An International Journal of Theory, Research and Practice, 1*(1), 39–53.

Relevant Sections: Coach-Client Matching

Purpose
- Explore factors that impact selection and matching of coaches with executives
- Focus on three factors
    1. Surface diversity factors: culture/race and gender
    2. Deep diversity factors: values and personality
    3. Experience

Design / Methodology
- Conceptual paper
- Presents selection and matching process model, which incorporates different phases
    - Set up: Client organization identifies executives and the coaching objectives
    - Choose providers: Client organization chooses coaching providers
    - Proposes coaches: Providers propose coaches to client
    - Select coaches: Client organization selects a pool of coaches
    - Create short list: Client organization matches two or three coaches to executive
    - Make final selection: Executive chooses the coach from short list
- Employs coaching and mentoring literature to support discussion of selecting and matching issues

Findings / Implications
- Argues focus should be on selecting high-quality coaches, not matching
- Suggests a need to support executives

      o Prepare executives for coaching experience
      o Provide support to executives in their matching decisions
- Inconclusive regarding matching criteria, perhaps favoring dissimilarity between coach and client

Originality / Value
- Systematic discussion of matching offers issues to consider
- Provides an organization's perspective

Strengths
- Defines terms: executive coaching, coach, executive coachee, client organization, selecting, matching
- Draws on mentoring literature to inform discussion
- Addresses the arguments for matching on similarities or differences
- Provides implications for coaching practice

Limitations
- Based on perspective; no empirical evidence to support arguments
- Many cited references appear also to be conceptual in nature
- Lacks interpretation of differences between mentoring and coaching

Categories: T1, I, C62, N15

Section 7. Additional Resources

In this section we have compiled a list of additional coaching resources, including coaching organizations that may be useful for readers. Although this list is not comprehensive and we do not necessarily endorse any of these particular sources, we wanted to direct readers to further coaching resources to supplement the articles that were included in this sourcebook.

Organizations Supporting Coaching Practice and Research

Association for Coaching (AC)
- Launched in 2002, AC is a London-based organization with the goal of promoting best practice and raising awareness and standards across the coaching industry.
- AC also distributes awards to recognize efforts made by organizations and students for outstanding contributions to practice and research in coaching ($500).
- www.associationforcoaching.com/home/index.htm

Australian Psychological Society Interest Group in Coaching Psychology (APS IGCP)
- Created in 2002, the IGCP, with more than 600 members, facilitates the theoretical, applied, and professional development of coaching psychology as an emerging theoretical and applied subdiscipline of psychology.
- www.groups.psychology.org.au/igcp

British Psychological Society Special Group in Coaching Psychology (BPS SGCP)
- The SGCP's aims are to promote the development of coaching psychology as a professional activity and to clarify the benefits of incorporating psychological approaches within coaching practice.
- SGCP supports coaching psychology research by sponsoring an annual research award as well as a practitioner's Achievement Award for distinguished contributions to coaching psychology ($400, invitation to attend European Coaching Psychology Conference).
- www.bps.org.uk/coachingpsy/coachingpsy_home.cfm

Center for Creative Leadership (CCL®)
- CCL focuses exclusively on leadership education and research, including executive coaching.
- CCL sponsors a number of awards to stimulate research and the application of research to the practice of leadership development.
- www.ccl.org

Graduate School Alliance for Executive Coaching (GSAEC)
- In 2006, GSAEC was formed to establish and maintain standards for education and training provided by academic institutions for the discipline and practice of executive coaching.
- www.gsaec.org

Global Coaching Community (GCC)
- Set up in response to the 2008 Dublin Global Coaching Convention, GCC is an evolving nonsolicitation social network platform for coaching stakeholders to share, explore, research, and collaborate.
- The 450-plus members, a fraction of the 15,000 coaches who have signed up to the Dublin Declaration on Coaching, collaborate within 25 discussion work groups supporting different coaching foci (e.g., education and development, research, small business, regional interests).
- gccweb.ning.com

The Institute of Coaching
- Established in 2009, the Institute of Coaching grew out of a partnership between The Coaching and Positive Psychology Initiative at McLean Hospital and The Foundation of Coaching (TFC), a project of the Harnisch Foundation, and is dedicated to enhancing the integrity and credibility of the larger field of coaching by advancing coaching research, education, and practice. The Institute of Coaching compiled a list of more than 200 graduate-level academic coaching programs in the United States, Canada, Australia, New Zealand, and the United Kingdom (see pennsurveys.org/coaching/?q=views/institutions for list of institutions).
- Continuing the TCF principles, The Institute of Coaching is committed to building a scientific foundation of coaching-related research, with $100,000 awarded annually in grants.
- www.instituteofcoaching.org

International Coach Federation (ICF)
- Formed in 1995 and with more than 14,000 members, ICF is the largest worldwide resource for professional coaches, dedicated to advancing the coaching profession, including executive and leadership coaching as well as other forms of coaching.
- ICF hosts the ICF Research Portal, at coachfederation.org, which includes the ICF Global Coaching Study (2007) and the ICF Global Coaching Client Study (2009) as well as other industry reports, research articles, and case studies.
- www.coachfederation.org

The Executive Coaching Forum (TECF)
- An outgrowth of routine meetings between Boston-area practitioners in 1999, The Executive Coaching Forum's stated mission is to advance the highest standards and best practices of executive coaching with all members of the coaching partnership.
- The most notable TECF resource is *The Executive Coaching Handbook,* written and revised by respected practitioners and used in more than 25 countries.
- www.theexecutivecoachingforum.com

Conferences

Conference	Sponsor	1st Annual Meeting
European Coaching Psychology Conference (National Coaching Psychology Conference)	BPS SGCP	2004
Executive Coaching Conference	University of Maryland	2009
Executive Coaching Conference	The Conference Board	
Global Coaching Convention	GCC	2008
ICF Coaching Research Symposium	ICF	2003
International Research Conference on Coaching		2008
Society of Industrial and Organizational Psychology Conference	SIOP	1985

Books

- Anderson, D., & Anderson, M. (2004). *Coaching that counts: Harnessing the power of leadership coaching to deliver strategic value.* Burlington, MA: Elsevier.

- Cavanagh, A., Grant, A., & Kemp, T. (Eds.). (2005). *Evidence-based coaching: Contributions from the behavioral sciences (Vol. 1).* Bowen Hills, Queensland, Australia: Australian Academic Press.

- Clutterbuck, D., & Hussain, Z. (2009). *Virtual coach, virtual mentor.* Charlotte, NC: Information Age Publishing.

- Executive Coaching Forum. (2008). *The executive coaching handbook: Principles and guidelines for a successful coaching partnership* (4th ed.). Executive Coaching Forum.

- Goldsmith, M., Lyons, L., & Freas, A. (Eds.). (2000). *Coaching for leadership: How the world's greatest coaches help leaders learn.* San Francisco, CA: Jossey-Bass/ Pfeiffer.

- Greif, S. (2007). Advances in research on coaching outcomes. *International Coaching Psychology Review, 3,* 222–247.

- Hart, E. W., & Kirkland, K. (2001). *Using your executive coach.* Greensboro, NC: Center for Creative Leadership.

- Hernez-Broome, G., & Boyce, L. A. (Eds.). (2010). *Advancing executive coaching: Setting the course for successful leadership coaching.* San Francisco, CA: Jossey-Bass.

- Hunt, J., & Weintraub, J. (2007). *The coaching organization: A strategy for developing leaders.* Thousand Oaks, CA: Sage.

- Kilburg, R. R., & Diedrich, R. C. (2007). *The wisdom of coaching: Essential papers in consulting psychology for a world of change.* Washington, DC: American Psychological Association.

- Kirkland Miller, K., & Hart, E. W. (2001). *Choosing an executive coach.* Greensboro, NC: Center for Creative Leadership.

- Palmer, S., & Whybrow, A. (2007). *Handbook of coaching psychology: A guide for practitioners.* New York: Routledge.

- Peterson, D. (2002). Management development: Coaching and mentoring programs. In K. Kraiger (Ed.), *Creating, implementing, and managing effective training and development* (pp. 160–191). San Francisco, CA: Jossey-Bass.

- Peterson, D., & Kraiger, K. (2004). A practical guide to evaluating coaching: Translating state-of-the-art techniques to the real world. In

J. Edwards, J. Scott, & N. Raju (Eds.), *The human resources program evaluating handbook*. Thousand Oaks, CA: Sage.

- Sperry, L. (2004). *Executive coaching: The essential guide for mental health professionals*. New York: Brunner-Routledge.

- Stober, D. R., & Grant, A. (2006). *Evidence based coaching handbook: Putting best practices to work for your clients*. Hoboken, NJ: John Wiley & Sons.

- Ting, S., & Scisco, P. (Eds.). (2006). *The CCL handbook of coaching: A guide for the leader coach*. San Francisco, CA: Jossey-Bass.

- Valerio, M. A., & Lee, R. J. (2005). *Executive coaching: A guide for the HR professional*. Hoboken, NJ: John Wiley & Sons.

- Underhill, B., McAnally, K., Koriath, J., & Goldsmith, M. (2007). *Executive coaching for results*. San Francisco, CA: Berrett-Koehler.

Coaching-Focused Publications

- *The Annual Review of High Performance Coaching and Consulting*
- *Coaching at Work*
- *Coaching: An International Journal of Theory, Research and Practice*
- *The Coaching Journal*
- *The Coaching Psychologist*
- *Consulting Psychology Journal: Practice and Research*
- *International Coaching Psychology Review*
- *International Journal of Coaching in Organizations*
- *International Journal of Evidence-based Coaching and Mentoring*
- *International Journal of Mentoring and Coaching*
- *The Journal of Coaching Education*

Bibliographies

- Douglas, C. A., & Morley, W. H. (2000). *Executive coaching: An annotated bibliography*. Greensboro, NC: Center for Creative Leadership.

- Grant, A. M. (2009). *Workplace, executive and life coaching: An annotated bibliography from the behavioural science and business literature (May 2009)*. Coaching Psychology Unit, University of Sydney, Australia.

Ordering Information

To get more information, to order other CCL Press publications, or to find out about bulk-order discounts, please contact
us by phone at +1 336 545 2810 or visit our online bookstore
at **www.ccl.org/publications**.

www.ingramcontent.com/pod-product-compliance
Lightning Source LLC
Chambersburg PA
CBHW062026210326
41519CB00060B/7183